Bouvier gives us a time-lapse view ▊▊▊ [barcode]
the Big Bang through the emerg T0267494
us) on to the present day, in which we are the aliens, and from
there into an amortal future. His intricate and stunningly beauti-
ful sentences are full of surprising scientific specificity. It's sleight
of hand at its most poetic.
—COLE SWENSEN, author of *Art in Time*

This is a marvelous book. Only an immensely fertile imagination
could tell so elemental a tale in so straightforward yet evocative
a fashion. Simple sentences often carry astounding weight. Bou-
vier makes one care about characters like "Life" and "We" and
then the emergence of virtually all of the world's major thinkers
in cameo. —CHARLES ALTIERI, UC-Berkeley

Geoff Bouvier has written a tour through physics and biology and
language and art and mathematics and sociology, to the point
where such categorizations fall away into meaninglessness, and
everything becomes, again, one. This book, like all great books,
reframes reality, imagines unbelievable true stories, and by doing
so creates for us a richer way of apprehending the world.
—PATRICK MADDEN, author of *Disparates*

An encyclopedic epic after Eduardo Galeano, *Us from Nothing* takes
on history in poetically compressed, paragraphic cantos. In conver-
sation with cosmic origins as it connects with patterns, past events
and pressing concerns, the whole corrects records, and delights in
telling a tale of the tribe. A contextualizing arrangement, part Blake,
part Williams, wholly relational and delighting. —HOA NGUYEN,
author of *A Thousand Times You Lose Your Treasure*

US FROM
NOTHING

Also by Geoff Bouvier

——

Glass Harmonica
Living Room

US FROM NOTHING

a poetic history

GEOFF BOUVIER

BLACK LAWRENCE PRESS

BLACK LAWRENCE PRESS

Executive Editor: Diane Goettel
Cover Art: "Genesis: Exile" by Marek Olszewski
Book Cover and Interior Design: Zoe Norvell

ISBN: 978-1-62557-071-0

Published 2024 by Black Lawrence Press.
Printed in the United States.

for Sindu

TABLE OF CONTENTS

13.8 Billion Years Ago: The Big Bang   1

13.6 Billion Years Ago: Stars   2

4.5 Billion Years Ago: Earth   3

3.8 Billion Years Ago: Life   4

443 Million Years Ago: Life on Land   5

66 Million Years Ago: End of the Dinosaurs   6

56 Million Years Ago: Mammals   7

7.5 Million Years Ago: Humans   8

3.3 Million Years Ago: Tools   9

1.5 Million Years Ago: Fire   10

300,000 Years Ago: Sapiens   11

220,000 Years Ago: Mass Migration   12

120,000 Years Ago: Music   13

100,000 Years Ago: Language   14

73,000 Years Ago: Extinction-Level Event   15

42,000 Years Ago: Mathematics   16

40,000 Years Ago: Art   17

30,000 Years Ago: Stories   18

16,000 Years Ago: Humans Everywhere   19

13,000 Years Ago: The Last Humans   20

12,000 Years Ago: Pets   21

10,000 Years Ago: Work   22

10,000 Years Ago: Civilization   23

8,000 Years Ago: Private Property   25

6,000 Years Ago: Cities   26

3200 Before Common Era: Writing   27

3100 Before Common Era: Money   28

3000 Before Common Era: Time   29

2700 Before Common Era: War   30

2300 Before Common Era: Empire   32

2100 Before Common Era: Law   32

1500 Before Common Era: Religion   34

1367 Before Common Era: Monotheism   35

1290 Before Common Era: Judaism   36

776 Before Common Era: Sports   37

600 Before Common Era: Evil and Salvation   38

542 Before Common Era: Taoism   39

539 Before Common Era: Civil Rights   40

508 Before Common Era: Democracy   41

479 Before Common Era: Confucianism   43

460 Before Common Era: Buddhism   44

399 Before Common Era: Atheism   46

370 Before Common Era: Science   47

240 Before Common Era: Geography   48

200 Common Era: Medicine   49

313 Common Era: Christianity   50

610 Common Era: Islam   52

723 Common Era: Clocks   53

850 Common Era: Gunpowder   54

1040: Advanced Science   56

1215: More Inclusive Civil Rights   57

1327: Humanism   58

1350: The Plague   59

1440: Printing Press   61

1444: Targeted Enslavement   62

1450: Capitalism   64

1522: Circumnavigation   65

1543: Heliocentrism   67

1597: Engineering   68

1600: Corporations   69

1604: Microscopes and Telescopes   70

1610: Astronomy   71

1644: Freedom of the Press   72

1666: Modern Cities   73

1687: Calculation   75

1712: Industrialization   76

1796: Vaccination   77

1800: Batteries   78

1814: Astrophysics   79

1821: Motors   80

1826: Photography   81

1831: Electromagnetism   83

1837: Telecommunications   84

1838: Mechanical Calculation   85

1839: Solar Energy   87

1842: Evolution   88

1842: Materialism   89

1846: Soap   90

1848: Communism   91

1867: Women Voting   92

1877: Sound Recording   93

1879: Light Bulbs   94

1886: Automobiles   96

1895: Motion Pictures   97

1900: Quantum Mechanics   98

1903: Powered Flight   99

1905: Relativity   100

1907: Plastics   101

1908: Nitrogen Synthesis   102

1927: Uncertainty Principle   103

1928: Antibiotics   104

1936: Computation   105

1945: The Bomb   106
1948: Universal Civil Rights   107
1952: DNA   108
1957: Global Positioning Systems   109
1958: Microtechnology   110
1960: Birth Control   111
1969: The Internet   112
1969: Moon Landing   113
2003: Human Genome   114
2008: Social Networks   115
Present Day: Aliens   116
Near Future: Technological Singularity   117
Near Future: Telepathy   118
Near Future: Amortality   119

Acknowledgments   121

13.8 Billion Years Ago: THE BIG BANG

Before the beginning, there was nothing – no size, no weight, no color, no shape – but the nothing was changing.

A nothing must enjoy a possibility. Perhaps the void, in its autonomy, grew lonely or bored. Perhaps whatever had no nature pondered nature, asking questions of its not-yet-self.

Tell us, neutral blank abyss, how we got from you to us.

At the very first moment, a brighter something unwraps from nothing, and all the energy releases like a supreme being's muscular twitch. A cosmos before us becomes matter and space.

Some say we still hear the changing void in joy or pain moaning *Om*. Others claim the universe was born crying for light.

13.6 Billion Years Ago: STARS

Scattered particles collect into hot molecular clouds everywhere for hundreds of thousands of years. And that's all that happens anywhere in the universe for hundreds of thousands of years.

Then the cloudy remnants gather enough heaviness, and a tremendous force unleashes. Atoms crack apart and fuse and crack apart and fuse, birthing energetic bodies of flaming nuclear bonds – self-sustaining spheres – the first stars.

New elements forge inside stars' massive cores. Helium. Lithium. More elements burst into being as old stars explode. Carbon. Oxygen. In time, the shattered bodies of the stars will make you and me and everyone and everything.

4.5 Billion Years Ago: EARTH

Cosmic cloud after cosmic cloud collapses in nuclear fusion. Every stellar ignition blasts elemental fragments into orbits where the molten matter cools and recombines as hurtling globes encircling newborn stars.

In one such solar system, around the infant Sun, an average iron stone with a strong inner churn turns too fast. Its first day passes after six hours. The cracking surface seethes and seems to melt. Its careening mass collides with other astral debris, gouging out a crater whose colossal divot flies and forms a moon.

A world is never certain, but for now, the third planet from the Sun spins here.

3.8 Billion Years Ago: LIFE

It's easy to argue that everything everywhere is alive — that we're all just variations of a self-reproducing, self-consuming, interrelated state of matter and antimatter — because every star, stone, person, and particle converts energy and settles into a bounded state driven to sustain its own bounded state, in cooperation with, and at the expense of, other bounded states.

It's also easy to argue that nothing anywhere is alive. That what was once considered life will be seen as just another property of everything — synthesizing, animating, reacting to its environment for a time, and eventually disorganizing.

As Empedocles will put it, in a few billion years — when the ethereal embryos of matter and energy grow efficient enough for consciousness, and consciousness arranges as culture, and culture matures into a Greek sage named Empedocles — "Life and death are mere questions of mixture and separation."

Vital acids may have rained to Earth from cosmic clouds, or proteins may have sprung from our own ocean vents. Either way, now the seafloors swarm with glowing orb-like protozoans.

Life exists because of sunlight, and life exists because of shade. For all of life's time on our planet, no cell has survived unless it swam below the canopy of water.

Oceans throng with microbes, sponges, corals, crabs, rays, mollusks, fish. For 3.4 billion years, their bodies have complicated and decomposed, and their slow decay has outgassed layers that dim the deadliness of the Sun.

Today, life has learned to hold a drop of ocean in its egg. New cells born on dry land can thrive above the water, breathing in the shaded air.

Life will only have to walk for an eighth as long as it swam before it thinks, looks back, and sees its dazed reflection in the sea.

A second star of morning glows eerie and faint, ominous sign on the dawn skyline. No tyrannosaurus is able to perceive it, twinkling like Venus, low in the rosy distance. And for hours, the sky's new morning "star" expands. Until it slams Earth's atmosphere – a flaming, five-mile-wide meteor plunging through haze, disintegrating oxygen, approaching touchdown.

When the big rock hits, vaporizing seawater, all life within six hundred miles is snuffed out by a thunderous force like billions of volcanoes thrusting rocks around as if they were glowing fluid. From the sudden crater, hill-sized tsunamis rise, as fast as hurricanes, threshing over seafloors, pushing beaches miles inland. A spreading fog brings rain of blazing tar that sets fire to forests. In days, an ashfall blanket drifts across the shorelines, choking ocean shallows into blackened mud. The planet spins encased in cloud.

Artificial winter lasts a million years. The final dinosaur exhales and lies still on dead land.

56 Million Years Ago: MAMMALS

Beneath the seas above future Texas, enormous oysters salivate white pearls that weigh a pound apiece. Antarctica's rains grow fertile jungles. An island settles into India, sliding slowly northward, marching into southern Asia, plowing the flatlands into towering Himalayas. Brown cones, green needles, clouds of spores, giant insects open the ways to crackling glades of brighter flowers, birds, and berries. Among nature's intense new colors, below the lowest grasses, we find ourselves. The first mammals.

Quick-witted, we combat famine by eating anything, resorting to trickery, scavenging, burrowing. Forced into hiding by adaptive predators and shifting climate, crawling through tunnels, we cultivate oily skins to manage inner temperatures, develop whiskers, hair, sharper vision, complex teeth. Our jaws refine to change vibrations into sounds. Warm bodies distill food for our babies. We nibble at the underbrush of an emergent ecosphere, sheltering broods inside our bellies.

7.5 Million Years Ago: HUMANS

Immense ice sheets thaw and retreat. Every summer warmer than the summer before. Much of Gondwanaland is a broad golden field of grasses waving between distant trees. Out in the open, every living thing is at risk of being eaten.

Here, an ape comes down from the leafy safe canopy in the morning. This ape is on two legs, trotting in a group, hefting rocks, finding hiding spots. Apes together, leaping, yelling, threaten even bears and big cats. Many apes are standing as one.

These apes are the first of us. *Orrorin.* The first humans.

Orrorin young imitate their elders. They dig with flat rocks, pick lice from each other's coats, return to the trees at dusk, fold down soft leaves, and weave night nests. Quicker to fresh kills – quicker than vultures – Orrorin cultivate a taste for pink meat. In time, there's hard enamel on their teeth.

Many will share the land with Orrorin. Ardipithecans' legs lengthen, Australopithecans' arms taper, Paranthropans' brains swell and complicate. Habilis sees in color, but not in the dark. Ergasters use pointy sticks to settle disputes. Erectus males and females mate face to face.

We'll all tread, stride, amble, sprint – and our minds and bodies will improve. But upright humans might never outrun apelike hungers, angers, or urges.

3.3 Million Years Ago: TOOLS

Those who stayed in trees are beasts to us now, squatting up there, fig juice on their faces, jabbering nonsense. They see how the river floods, but we can read its anger. Night is where their danger is, but we appease darkness. Dreaming shows us worlds behind the world. We feel the wind's awareness, how it bites and shrieks. Sometimes, rotted fruit pulp makes us dizzy, and we laugh and laugh until we fall asleep.

Our hands are free. We pick up stones to heave at bears. We peel the lengths of sticks against our teeth to smooth them. Smoother sticks in earthen holes come bristling up with tasty mites. Flint from chalky cliffs will flake an edge across a darker rock, an edge to shave off skins and hack the flesh from bones. Pounding with a boulder cracks an antelope skull. The pudding inside skulls is delicious. At camping sites, streamside, strips of tree bark carry water. We pile snug shelter, thatching branches.

The ones who stayed in trees use rough implements, but special tools encourage new skills. Technology advances us, yet makes us more savage. Technology outpaces our genes.

1.5 Million Years Ago: FIRE

Crooked lightning flashes this fast fiend to life. We track its black smoke toward a ravenous face, not too close. With branches, we might grab the writhing monster. A nest of wood can keep its bright offspring. But fires have to eat throughout the night, and unexpected rain reduces flame to so much char.

Who was it? Agni, Māui, Prometheus, Coyote, Lo Hsüan, Grandmother Spider, Azazel? Who first possessed the hot shining air all living things fear? Perhaps a modest toolmaker, some Erectus squatting in a copse, clacking rock against rock, sparked a dry tuft of grass, raising tendrils of smoke.

From here on, fire will work for us, to chew the bulk of what we eat. It defangs our food. Before, the night threw frightful shadows that could kill us. Now, we get to sleep wherever. Or stay awake, acquainting with each other and the dark. Over winters, fire's warmth adapts us anyplace. For many generations, we will whisper in the heated light, inventing myths and rhythms.

Once we control fire, humanity leaps from scavenger to predator. Lions, wolves, eagles – other top hunters – have evolved courageous, fearless, self-secure. But fire too quickly grants ungainly majesty. By fire, we earn alchemy, chemistry, weaponry, internal combustion, even freedom from Earth. And still our existence feels anxious and stressed. Like each new success is feasting upon us.

300,000 Years Ago: SAPIENS

The first *Homo sapiens sapiens* is a child of two who aren't like her. They make no sense to her. No one understands. The other children leave her out and play adult. Over grasslands, sunny days, no one grooms her. In the water pools, her weird face reflects. She sprouts no hair across her shoulders, none upon her chest. Longer head-hair hangs unseemly. She is ugly. Eyes too wide. We see her milking places. No male sniffs her. She hides herself with hoods, thick furs, even in summer. She turns her gaze to mask a thought and sees how others blink, blink without thinking. All they do is eat, sleep, wash, make waste, stare at fire, fight, produce offspring. She has to dig a deeper pit inside herself for feelings. *I'm the first of my kind. I must not be the last.*

220,000 Years Ago: MASS MIGRATION

Sapiens stand and scan horizons. We live to visit every edge. North's a waste of sun and sand. The rest ends in water.

Now the weather worsens every year. Air becomes an icy vise. It drives us away. We outrun starvation, tracking mammoth and bison for days across mudflats that once were seas.

Beyond the reedy shores, outside the plains of home, we find lush, unexpected lands. Our children's great-grandchildren hunt and sing in leafy warm places. Denisovans, Sapiens, Neanderthal, all humans: exploring idyllic valleys, settling near cows, corn, salmon, figs.

When we meet again, thousands of generations after glaciers stop chasing us, we'll hardly recognize each other.

120,000 Years Ago: MUSIC

Long before we speak or write, we start to hear a natural song, as though the universe forever hums a patient, urgent message, and we've learned to play its tune. We understand how Sun and Moon arrive and pass, gazelles and grass show up then leave, summers fall into winters then bloom into springs, and everybody dies. Around our fires, we practice nature's measures, and we move without a reason, just to move. It reminds us we share an invisible body, singing as our heartbeats synch along, developing a rhythmic sense of flowing time. Music composes us.

Many creatures force rude noises from their throats – cries at birth, calls against predators, purrs of trust, grunts of disgust. We move our lips and tongues and breathe across the mouth-shapes we might make. But no expression's ever been a word.

Then a newborn Sapiens cries from the back of a cave, heralding evolution.

The child ages, generating meaningful syllables. Members of the clan can't sing along with this one. Perhaps they should kill it, this unusual youth whose gibberish chills them, whose voice sirens sleep-visions awake.

I'm the first person with a name. Primal Poet. Safe Mutant.

I'm the first to name another. Loving-Mother-of-the-New-Order. Friend-Who-Stayed-When-I-Was-Weird.

I whisper the first prayer. Please listen.

Other people dance, feel, kill, and dream. But this one's brain is built for grammar, prepared to transmit.

We relay information, roughly spoken and soon forgotten unless violently enforced. *Only eat when you're hungry. Only do what you can do. Only be with those you know.* A supervolcano's exploding, wounding the planet – a violent hot start to nine hundred years of global winter. Many will shiver short lifetimes without seeing sunlight. Every last Erectus dies. A few cooperating Sapiens huddle in darkened valleys, suffering decades, starving, brushing ash from their faces. It's almost the end of us.

At the supereruption site, ocean water pours into a yawning crater, a torrent filling a future mountain lake. Two thousand generations later, Toba's lolling shores recall our almost Armageddon – blue, blue calm on a tropical island. It might take catastrophes to remind us we're cousins.

The Sun always rises. Plant growth echoes the cycle of seasons. Lockstep tides follow strict Moon phases.

Scratched into bones, we total our days. Pick *one* red berry. Pick *two*. Eat *more*. We eye sized portions of barley, rationing fairly. In branches of lindens, we estimate crows. In shallow pools, the minnows.

We count on the parts of our finite physiques. Ten fingers add to ten toes. Twenty equals *one body*. Every body reaches, weighs, and measures out an odd connection with its numbers.

Mathematics reframe reality, telling unbelievable true stories. Maths express ideas our minds must bend to form – irrationality, negativity, symmetry. Wild tales of change and shape, epic quests that help us touch the surface of the Moon.

Nature functions, integrates, generalizes, differentiates what nobody's body can easily sense, as though remaining-strange-to-us were a condition of existence. The square root of negative one red berry is *imaginary*. The universe's secrets are related to us by mathematical increments.

40,000 Years Ago: ART

We drag sticks in the sand, carving grains into lines. Arrange curious stones – not to use, just to see. Some kick at them.

The elders guard a cliff where red-tinted rock drips. Its mud dyes our skin. We express ourselves with reddish marks the dried mud makes.

Dangerous nights, fire-shadows lace the cavern walls. We're spellbound by blazes. Mornings, ashen fingers sketch a fire's gestures.

Last night's hot light showed us something no one's eyes have seen before and words can't yet explain – shadows shaped like animals! It was unfamiliar medicine. Today we traced a pinch of ash and reddish clay to stripe the walls with marks that look like more than marks. We drew some bison flattened out so they could live like herds of shadow bison on the walls.

We showed the elders. All they saw were marks of reddish clay.

Then the medicine caught up to them. Our marks came half-alive like captured bison in their eyes.

30,000 Years Ago: STORIES

We harvest river ferns, peel their skins, dry out fibers in the sun, and gossip as we grind the fibers into powders. We whip the powders into paste, shape the pasty bits to loaves, then place loaves inside fires. Later we may come together and break bread.

We drink the juice of rotted figs as fatherly Sun goes over, motherly moonlight follows, and stars express the quiet endless dramas of the sky. Our holy seers chant and dance until they lay their bodies down to let their spirits fly.

At dawn, our seers wake with images and words to ward or welcome what their spirits left to find. Last night they walked among the clouds, above the falling rain. Then they breathed among the whales beneath the ocean. Today they speak to us with otherworldly voices, and we paint each other's faces, and we lace our throats with ornamental beads to prove we listen.

Humans seem related to another world, but only holy seers travel back from there to here. That other world is where we go to die, and where our holy seers make diseases disappear. While we're alive, our seers deal with threat before it threatens. They can understand the wind's opinions. Our seers help us speak in nature's speech. They tie us to another world, and tell us tales that show us who we are and why we're here.

16,000 Years Ago: HUMANS EVERYWHERE

We've learned to kill, clean, freeze, and store the creatures we call *game*. Using sewing needles carved of bone, we layer furs over skins, coating ourselves in purloined warmth. We chisel shelters out of ice, keeping winter fires high with dung and blubber.

As glaciers thaw, we wander far.

To the hoofed, clawed, or taloned unsuspecting, a person's just a loping, vocal creature with sticks and rocks in its paws. Goodbye, giant sloths, woolly mammoths, sabretooths, passenger pigeons. The alpha apex predator is going global.

13,000 Years Ago: The Last Humans

For over seven million years, the human family has included many species. Orrorin, Australopithecus, Habilis, Erectus, Ergaster, Denisovan, Neanderthal, Idaltu – all have lived, thrived, and eventually died out.

Now, on an island Indonesians will call Pulau and the Portuguese will rename Flores, the last archaic human species encounters the self-proclaimed Knowing Man. We Sapiens land in longboats and find the green lagoons and palm-lined shores wholly hospitable. Never mind the small people prospering, loving, and carving communities there, Floresiensis families hiding in their homes and in the hills. Tiny warriors standing four feet, weighing ninety pounds in cured skins, can't match the mighty Sapiens. We massacre every Floresiensis in a week.

One human species remains, with no equal enemy. Until aliens, microbes, a meteor, or the climate attacks, Sapiens will have to fight among ourselves.

12,000 Years Ago: PETS

Night eyes glow in darkness. Snarls echo outside circles of firelight. We must relieve ourselves in pairs, standing guard with spears. From the forest, howling chills us.

Those furry creatures share our spirit, or so the holy seers teach, but that won't save us. We hunt for similar meat. We'd even eat each other.

The generations go by.

Then a thin one comes in from the dark and whimpers for scraps. We throw bones to it. Soon we're feeding more of them. They break from their packs and follow when we migrate in winter.

Now there's the wild wolves who growl and stay proud in the cold, and the trained ones beside us who grovel. Our trained wolves help us track and hunt. They protect us and we feed them. Together we fix the luck of the chase.

We capture, keep, and eat the lambs, goats, cows, pigs. Cats can offer pest control and petulant companionship. Oxen enhance our strength. Silk moths dress us finely. Elephants fortify the military. Bees bring sweet honey. Camels, asses, horses, llamas carry us and our goods. Our flocks are living larders of warming hides, flowing milks, useful dung. Every other being on Earth shall live to serve the dominant human.

10,000 Years Ago: WORK

Among animals, we're chosen. Among plants, the choice is grass – waving hair of the land, embodiment of patience. For millions of years, green and golden grasses have covered a third of Earth's surface. Nothing transforms our star's energy as efficiently. Nothing so powerful was ever so humble.

Ever since passive-seeming grasses appeared, their whispering collective has steered the fate of earthly life. Grasses isolated forests. Grasses feed the wild herds. Grasses summoned apes to leave the overstory, compelling us to stand and walk on two feet.

Barley, corn, oat, rice, wheat, sugar, person. Together, we'll invent the sickle, the plow, pesticide, fertilizer, the tractor, the combine harvester, irradiation, genetic modification, and there shall be no day of rest. Backs and stalks bent over in noble shared labor.

All of us are only puppets to the grass.

For millennia we wandered, briefly sheltered, carried our belongings, and followed the food. Year round, we lived equally under the Sun and Moon, helped each other hunt and gather, and kept potential bullies in line.

Now instead we've settled beside the resources, an excess of resources, ploughing then sowing in soils near wide rivers. At home in warm places, we've structured walls of clay with roofs of sticks and woven reeds. Mice, cats, rats, sparrows, pigeons, insects self-domesticate to eat and breed among the-people-among-the-people. Together, we store the plants and herds, and protect the surplus of their varied products. We've named our places: Ain Mallaha, Göbekli Tepe, Mohenjo-daro. We've enjoyed our feasts of roasted sheep and goat, braised fowl, fried fish, warm bread, soft and hard cheeses, fluffy rice, butter cakes, shaved coconut, sweet puddings, fresh herbs, dried spices, boiled maize, pomegranates, yams, almonds, onions, olives, peaches, leeks, hot peppers, bananas, honey, figs. And from today, our lives reset around the Sun and seasons.

We've begun forgetting ancient ceremonies of the Moon. Men become the gatherers, as well as hunters, and women lose their equal standing, reduced to childbearing. Bullies rise, thieve, rent, pillage, tax, tithe, demand tributes, and soon we'll call them lords. It's the first of the priest-kings, first of the holy men who wield holiness as power. Our opinions clash to form new cultures. *Magic seems real. From here, the world looks flat. The gods exist and must be feared.* Population density brings collective identity. *What would other people think? What will everyone say?* Most will go along to get along. Trade routes, travel hubs, bargain for barter, fair exchange. No one knows all the skills anymore. It's the birth of the specialist, birth of charisma. Birth of the doomed-in-the-wild-but-now-viable, of the child who disobeys but lives, of the juvenile delinquent. Generational disconnect. Manufactured conflict. Declaration of war between rich and poor.

8,000 Years Ago: PRIVATE PROPERTY

Dragging staffs in the dirt, we draw proper lines. Between our drawn lines, some decide, this belongs. O land where we live, you frame what is good. Our temples, our hovels, our hearths, our stables, grain plots of our priests, parcels of planted vegetables – whatever lies within our lands, belongs.

Some impose this landed idea, border it, and enforce it, and now we all shall live to tend you, private property, and pass you on from god to priest to king to businessman, from father to son, territory to country, city-state to nation-state, individual to company to corporate entity, rich man to rich man to rich man.

Our bodies are based on physiques of fish. Our brains remain lizard. Our habits, ape.

But we've learned to augment our development. Art alters minds. Words connect us. We collaborate with grass and wolf to stave off hunger and predator. And with heat extending our power to modify matter, humans are becoming titans.

We fire bricks, forge metals, dig sewer systems, redirect rivers, roll on wheels, place trades, arrange wars. Side by side, expanding populations settle in the Indus River Valley, Egypt, Sumer, Peru. Whoever owns the land controls the food.

Over the years, our bodies begin to shrink and weaken, as humankind collects intelligence and quickens and strengthens. Yearning, afraid, with common purpose, we learn to coexist and serve as neighbors, competing, cooperating, and whispering behind our hands about each other.

"Good morning." It's Kushim, proud Sumerian, honored Uruki accountant. Today, Kushim will pray for Inanna's grace as he shuffles the dusty streets to visit taxpayers. At every house, he sharpens his reeds, wedges the points into wet clay slabs, and indents lines that take a whole day to harden, even in sun.

It's the real Year One. The dawn of fact. First moment in history. The beginning of collective memory. From this day forward, we are being recorded.

Kushim documents the matters of the state, with no statesman present. He documents transactions of the Leaders of the Plow, the Leaders of the Lambs, the Leaders of the Law, and the other leaders, grain-grinders, metalworkers, potters, butchers, bakers, brewers, ditchdiggers, sewage-haulers, taxpayers all. Kushim documents our goods and provisions, our cows, geese, goats, pigs, barley bushels, carven beads, and bits of bronze. He documents the priest-kings' plots of land.

In five thousand years, we'll still be reading Kushim's words, though the hand he used to write them no longer moves.

Barley smells nutty, sweet. Its fragrance infuses the air of Mesopotamia. Sumerians have always hulled its seeds, cooked up heady stews, and dried whole stalks to soak in barrels for malt.

Now the priests of Ninlil shall decree barley the blood of society, and the barley flows in bundles from farmers to servants to merchants: a go-between for services and goods. Before, a singer sang for beer, a cobbler traded shoes to eat a butcher's meat, a barber sheered a head to dress in shepherd's wool or sleep the night in bed. But this new priestly sorcery – money – makes exact change out of songs, food, shoes, clothing, shelter, even sex and salvation.

Money conjures real currency from simple barley, turns all to commodity, and leads us by an invisible hand into debt, talents, debt, shekels, debt, mina, debt, staters, debt, dollars, debt, drachmas, debt, rupees, debt, yen, debt, bitcoin, debt.

A Sumerian man extends an arm, palm faced outward, as if to motion *stop*, except he's measuring. Up and down the middle of the sky, the Sun's path over Sumer equals twelve hand-lengths. Call those dozen lengths of hands *the hours*.

Sumerians also tally hours on the ground. Upright objects in daylight throw consistent shadows. Draw a ring around a twig, divide the circle into twelves. From dawn, the Sun will dial along a dozen hand-length hours.

For a million generations, every life has led through luck and strife to random death. But now, we're telling time. We script a human regulation to nature's open rhythm.

2700 Before Common Era: WAR

Yesterday we men of Elam and Sumer waved hello along the roads and labored side by side in irrigation ditches.

Tomorrow we must rise as mortal enemies, arriving at a chosen field to try to end each other's lives.

Farewell, wives. Farewell, sons and daughters. We may never see you in this life again.

At dawn beneath the rising Sun, perhaps for the final time, our battle calls unblock our throats and we rush forward.

Around us sharp objects fly. Blizzards of spikes bury in skulls, shoulders, chests. *May the gods be proud of us!*

Shrieking survivors advance, propelling spears and stones, killing other men and breaking their limbs.

Let our names be remembered and our memories be loved! Warriors couple toe to toe, swinging blades, clubs, fists.

Our blows and counterblows, cloven muscles, slashed skins, opened wounds, exposed bones, necks disjointed.

Faces fear-twisted, red sprays of blood, spilling innards, whispered last words. *I was a young man. I never got to know who I am.*

Chaos, torsos split, flesh hanging, abhorrent smells, terrified eyes, last cries, splintering bone-sound.

Death screams, destroyed lives, collapsing humans crawling on a gore-slicked field, achieving . . . something.

A seeming eternity of confused minutes, until the men still standing come from only one side of the disagreement.

A victory is won for the priest-kings, their homelands, and their standards.

The weapons of dead people spoil the victors. And the Elams and Sumers of the world return to temporary peace.

So we solve our worst disputes. Our species is always at war with itself.

When gods outlined earthly boundaries, their ink was oceans, deserts, rivers, mountains.

Strangely conceived, born somewhere in secret, then set adrift in a basket of rushes and discovered downriver by humble gardeners, an anonymous orphan Jewish boy grows up in Akkad, the fearsome military state, and later becomes Akkad's mighty king. With his chosen new name, Sargon, and an army of thousands, he merges populations into one identity – *Akkadians*.

Sargon gives the Akkadians safe highways, a postal system, expanded trade, fair taxation. In return, his citizens lose their cherished ceremonies and mother tongues. If they organize uprisings, Sargon's army crushes them. Enheduanna, Sargon's daughter, becomes the world's first author. *My king, your lustrous lapis beard hangs down in profusion.*

As a profusely bearded king redraws lines between lands, his strokes become borders and the cost is blood.

Before the law stands humanity, in self-judgment. If innocence, then freedom. If crime, then punishment. In this wise way, social control softens: more secular, less fierce. Not whatever gods decree, or swords enforce, but what a person *writes*.

And we try to write into law the banishment of violence and strife. Also, the standardization of weights and measures. Also, monthly temple expenses, to be paid in barley, butter, goat, or sheep.

Among the laws of Ur-Nammu – great warrior-king and bringer of justice to Sumer, Akkad, and Ur – are these:

If you steal from my house, then I may have you sealed alive inside a wall of my house.

If you buy gold, silver, slave, sheep, ox, ass, or anything without witness or contract, then you are a thief, and you shall be put to death.

If a flood destroys your fields, then you may wash your debt-tablet in that water, and pay no rent for one year.

If a holy woman opens a tavern door, then she shall be burned in the public square.

If a husband finds his wife in congress with another, he may forgive her, but if he does, then both are forgiven. Instead, he may have them tied up face to face and thrown into a river, where he may watch them writhe and drown.

Nature has sung to us since long before we learned to hum along. We heard, and then we listened, and eventually we thought we understood. Nature's voices came disguised as thunder, fire, music, stories, the constellations, numbers – a host of unseen forces singing behind the seen.

Then as we came to babble with each other, we talked over nature, refining what we sensed into absolute figures. Beyond the actual mountains, there was a being who embodied mountains. Above the mere sky, a god of skies. And as we felt less godlike ourselves, we displaced our beliefs into abstract idols – a master of healing, a bringer of destruction, overseers of fertility and wisdom. In time, imaginations populated with pantheisms.

Now the Kuru people of northern India are thriving in a pantheistic society, chanting poems and prayers to their various deities. They call their holy words the Vedas, and they write the Vedas down. The Vedas outline medical practices that remain advanced for millennia. Their systematic grouping of humans into castes will haunt us in perpetuity. Western colonizing philosophers will plunder Vedic concepts: karma (reaping what you sow), dharma (the right way to live), moksha (liberation from time). Vedic religion will adapt into Hinduism, the final prehistoric faith still preaching to the monotheistic age.

Every cult in Egypt preaches balance, but the temple of the air god Amun has been tipping the scales. Amun's priests possess more land and cattle than anyone, including Pharaoh. Whose laws must good Egyptians follow? Amun's, or Pharaoh's?

Magnificent Pharaoh, as if in self-defense, invents a god above the others, who manifests among us as our shining Sun. Pharaoh rechristens the Sun *Aten*, and assumes the name *Akhenaten* in service to this god of gods.

And in service to Aten, Akhenaten gathers supporters, Egypt's fan-bearers, the national wealth, a thousand people he's enslaved, and his favorite wife and youngest son, and the Egyptian army escorts a vast caravan away from Thebes to a capital city that doesn't exist yet.

As the enslaved of Egypt erect a grand edifice to Aten, Akhenaten issues executive orders and raves religious poetry. *Those on Earth come from your hand as you made them.* His unfree workers toil, glistening spires rise, and Akhenaten revels in religious visions. *When you dawn, we live. When you set, we die.*

Inking his words onto scrolls of papyrus, Akhenaten leaves behind all matters of the state. The citizens of the world's most prosperous nation rebel and riot. Akhenaten's soldiers march back into Thebes, closing Amun's temples, hacking sacred icons off the walls, collecting idols for public burning. Executive order: no other gods exist besides Aten. Executive order: no likeness of Aten has eyes or a face.

With each fresh day, our born-again Aten gleams. A heretical prophet-king rebrands himself as sole medium between human and Heaven. Executive order: convert or be killed.

Strangely conceived, born somewhere in secret, then set adrift in a basket of rushes and discovered downriver by the pharaoh's daughter, an anonymous orphan Jewish boy grows up in the comfort of the Great House in the capital of Egypt. His prophetic career begins decades later with a justified murder, subsequent exile, and a fit of hopeless desolation on the top of a mountain that manifests as flame and a voice calling him to his life's mission.

This man's fiery muse reveals itself as The-One-Who-Causes-to-Be, a loving, punishing, almighty God, capital *G*, who prods him: Go down, Moses, and give the Word that will lead your people out of servitude.

Moses descended, freed a nation from bondage, authored five profound books, and preached ethics and law for the rest of his days. *An eye for an eye, a tooth for a tooth.*

Whether Moses was a man or many men, there will never be a more influential poet. The words ascribed to that name mark a moral guideline for three thousand years. *Honor your parents, take a day of rest each week, no killing, no lying, no swearing, no stealing or wanting to steal, no adultery or wanting adultery, no other gods than the One.*

Whether Moses was a man or many men, he or they united six hundred thousand enslaved people into an army of monotheists who rose against oppression, escaped between the frothing waves of a tidal sea, and seized liberty.

Yesterday we men of Athens and Sparta stabbed at each other with spears and slashed at each other with swords.

Tomorrow we shall awaken as cordial competitors and arrive at the chosen field in Elis to contend at sports.

Farewell, wives. Farewell, sons and daughters. We shall return, and when we do, we hope to bring home glory, wealth, and fame.

At dawn on the first day of the festival of Zeus, a call fills the throats of the crowd – *Diagoras! Leonidas! Chionis! Milo!*

And these men and others race armored and naked, in chariots and on foot. They jump, box, and wrestle naked.

They throw discuses and javelins, and display the godlike abilities of humanity's most able bodies.

The swiftest runner at the first ceremonial games is a lithe chef named Koroibos.

One evasive boxer, Melankomas, avoids violence, earning the crown of olive leaves without heaving punches.

The Olympic Games refine soldiers, who were forced to fight to the end, into athletes who may play to win.

A youthful Persian truth-seeker crouches by a fire at the mouth of a cave where he's slept in solitude for weeks. Daily, the magus fasts and thinks, meditating on death, anger, difficulty, famine, war, disease, spoken lies, personal deceit, and the terrors of his own imagination. Building superhot, longer-burning fires, he conducts experiments and discovers new properties of heated materials. At night, among the mountains, he feels comfort under herds of stars.

The more the precocious magus experiments and ponders, the more he wrestles with despair. And tonight, in a fit of hopeless desolation, he stares into his blaze and swears he sees a humanoid form arise, menacing the smoke. It's fearsome, huge, smells sulphurous, and glows like dark magma. A voice hisses out of its charred face, "I am the embodiment of wickedness. Henceforth, I shall bring grave evil to this place."

The magus leaps to his feet. "No, Prince of Darkness! The Lord of Light and Truth exists to vanquish you!"

Thus speaks Zarathustra, first summoner of the Devil and accidental founder of Hell.

The story goes, Laozi was born an old man after sixty-two years in the womb. They say he wrote his lessons only when border police harassed him with strips of bamboo and bottles of ink. *If you overesteem great men, people become powerless. If you overvalue possessions, people begin to steal. Practice not-doing, and everything will fall into place.*

His times are beset by state-controlled mass ignorance, national security issues, unfair tax collection, continuous war, struggles for resources, and systems that enslave the poor and favor the rich. Adults entrench in old ways while the youth seek progress. Social policies worsen the lives of many while improving the means of a very few, who write the laws, after all. Students and progressives yearn for uncorrupted ideas and smarter leaders who'll free us to imagine more creative lives.

Laozi himself may or may not have breathed air, loved his parents, felt the soreness of age, or thought about our troubled world. Like Zarathustra in Persia, Moses and Abraham in Israel, Krishna in Mathura, and even more-storied mystics to come, the remembered name *Laozi* might signify a man, or it may refer to an avatar, an amalgam, a human ideal.

Nevertheless, Laozi's teaching on the way to virtue – the Tao – inspires centuries of spiritual and social justice, introduces us to the concepts of interdependence of opposites (yin and yang) and going with the flow (wu-wei), and shows us how to craft our thought into an art.

Insecure about his empire's greatness, the Babylonian king decrees his neighbors the Jews must pay tribute to him. When the Jewish king refuses this tax, Babylon seizes Jerusalem. Tens of thousands of Jewish citizens, forced from their homes, relocate and become slaves to the wealthy elite of Babylon. Jewish children and their children's children are born enslaved.

      After forty years of servitude, the Babylonian Jews awaken in a city under attack. Siege engines, war elephants, and the Persian army of Cyrus gather outside Babylon's invincible walls. But Cyrus' siege is a feint to buy time. As his soldiers encircle the city, his engineers dig causeways upriver from where the wide Tigris runs between the invincible walls of Babylon.

      At Cyrus' signal, the Tigris chokes to a trickle. Persian soldiers invade along the draining riverbed, stealing between the invincible walls into Babylon. The city falls by sundown.

      With the spoils of war before him, Cyrus commits unprecedented acts. He releases the Jewish people and escorts them to their homeland. He asserts equality among Persians, Babylonians, and Jews. He declares that all may choose their own religions.

      These protections and opportunities are carved into a rod-shaped rock. The Cyrus Cylinder becomes our first charter of personal freedom.

Many places, many years before a single word was written down, some charismatic humans assumed that gods had granted them godlike authority, and that this assumed grace could be passed to their sons and to their sons' sons. And along these lines ever since, people have organized society by oligarchy – "divine" clout of the elites – or by tyranny – brute force of the military.

Now a third option arrives in the form of a loud man who rides into the commons, another raver, but clean in crimson pleats and drapery, a resident of the capital. "I am Cleisthenes of Athens!" he calls. "Hear what I have to say!"

He hops from his horse to a spot in the square, stoops down to scoop up a handful of dirt, and we, the populace, gather.

"This earth," Cleisthenes says, as dark dust sifts between his fingers, "this earth is *yours*. You live upon it. Work in it. This soil mothers your creatures, your plants, your gods, yourselves. There's nothing it doesn't give and hasn't given!"

Cleisthenes of Athens has earned our attention.

"Here, I tell you, your land is prepared to lavish you with more. This place where you live can protect you, like the walls of a fortress, rising up. Together, you and this place can share a collective voice. A voice heard all the way to the halls of policy. It's called *governance by democracy!*"

"Democracy! Democracy!" our voice hails back, as though the land has amplified us.

"Till this day, you've been managed by muscle and trickery!" Cleisthenes thunders. "Priests and the rich have ruled you by force. Instead, we will persuade them to practice democracy. We can all participate in our own destinies!"

And along these lines ever since, trying to organize society by democracy, we've lapsed into oligarchy or tyranny.

Confucius lectures from a rolling ox cart. Even his measured gestures and tone of voice seem wise. He teaches in images. *The loose strand destroys the whole fabric. To move a mountain, begin by carrying stones.* Students follow on foot, tripping over each other, falling into the mud to absorb the master's words.

Confucius says that generational knowledge is more important than life experience, and generational knowledge must be preserved. His lifestyle seems like critique. He wears linen to spare silkworms, drinks no milk to keep calves with their mothers, shoots no birds unless they're in flight, and talks politely to all. He champions organization, stability, free education, just governance. Confucius shuns prayer, worship, gods that act like us, the concept of immortality. His tutorial might be called *How the World Conserves Itself.*

The man's exhausting – smarter than we are, judgmental, too exacting – but he demands no more of others than he can also do. His students practice altruism, observe social hierarchy, recite hundreds of passages from memory, and fire arrows true with their eyes closed. In fifty years, three thousand scholars enroll. Just seventy-two graduates can do as Confucius does.

The ancient kings of Babylon told abiding humanity how to be good by drafting hundreds of laws. Later, Moses in Egypt edited the code of ethics down to ten inspired commands. Now Confucius boils the essence of conscience into a single golden meaning. *Don't do unto others what you don't want them to do to you.*

Born laughing on satin pillows, prophesied a great man, raised in the seat of such privilege that he never feels hot or cold and never touches dust or dampness, Prince Siddhartha Gautama sheds no real tears until, at twenty-nine, he's stricken with a new emotion. On his first-ever excursion outside palace grounds, Siddhartha sees a state of affairs that changes him: an old man hobbling, a sick woman dying, religious suppliants begging for aid from another world, a fly-ridden corpse. Reality stuns him.

Horrified, confused, and ultimately moved, Siddhartha rejects his royal coddling, and strikes out empty-handed to wander the broken world. To understand abundance, he believes that he must suffer.

Siddhartha chops his hair, takes almost no food, rejects pleasure, and refocuses his thinking. But instead of finding enlightenment, he feels like he's trying to tie the air into knots. Six years pass as the prince wanders in self-sacrifice.

About to resign his quest, he relaxes and indulges. Siddhartha eats his first full meal since the palace days, a feast of mangoes with warm bread. He enjoys a bath in the pool of a river, and sits beneath a shade tree to reflect.

For the second time in his life, Siddhartha sees a state of affairs that changes him. With his inner eye he sees how time passes by gathering and dispersing. He sees abundance and suffering as parts of an interdependent whole. He sees the best life served by slowing down, breathing, and mindfully realizing.

The prince's face shines. Removing the veil of his ignorance, he discovers a middle way between excess and abstinence. Siddhartha is the Buddha now.

He returns to his kingdom to instruct whoever will listen: don't look beyond existence, don't crave some unknown creator, we only solve our suffering here and now.

"Never since thinking was raised to an art form has a thinker thought as artfully as Socrates." Or so says the Oracle at Delphi, which, for early Greeks, renders the claim a fact. But Socrates, with his curious gaze and wide eyes, works to prove the given facts wrong. His technique for doing so – questioning, analyzing, simplifying, then questioning again – applies to any divergent system of thought. Socrates challenges Greek elders, out-reasons Greece's best reasoners, interrogates words with inquisitive words, and pries open belief in the name of contemplation. He says we must try to know ourselves, and he champions logic as the mode to be good and live well. His tutorial might be called *How the World Progresses*.

Socrates' teachings irritate the social order. He teases Athenians for following gods instead of thinking for themselves, which is heresy. Charged with impiety, Socrates asks his accusers, "What are gods, if not people with grand goals and big ideas?" The voting majority answers, "Execute him!"

Socrates, annoying social gadfly, enrages the religious and the rich, and won't admit that nonconformity is bad for society. Condemned to die, our wisest drinks his poison among his friends, sacrificing life for truth.

For one brief moment, recorded later by Plato, the freethinking of a person outshines the groupthink of the state.

The sky's a moody god whose feelings cast the weather. The Sun is another god's chariot wheel. The Moon wears a smiling, motherly face. The Earth's a wide, flat, stationary place at the center of everything. Everything was crafted by someone like us, but supreme. Our maker's perfect creation is nature.

For hundreds of thousands of years, we imagine exclusionary narratives, act upon unlikely theories, inspire lasting works, and try to lift people above life's mysteries and difficulties. We tell ourselves we're standing over all that can be known, on the basis of our often-baseless stories.

As China's divided states wage war among the Hundred Schools of Thought, a logician from the School of Names employs his military genius for peace, preaches universal love, and inspires many followers. Mozi the master practices a method for recognizing truth from superstition: *observation, verification, application.* This scientific process lays a foundation firmer than fiction. Mozi teaches us to come down from standing over what we think we know, and instead to work to understand.

Every person is a temporary upright extension of the Earth's wide body. To appreciate our earthly body's interdependence, and to recognize the shape of our terrestrial self, it takes an all-around Greek scholar with a simple stick, and some bematists.

Of average height, bematists walk along the streets, mountains, deserts, fields, riverbanks, and shorelines evenly, counting their own even steps. Using bematist data, Greeks and Egyptians estimate great distances, usually for taxation purposes.

The all-around Greek scholar, Eratosthenes, chief librarian of Alexandria, has seen the Sun shine without shadows at noon in a far-off city on the summer solstice. The following year in Alexandria, Eratosthenes plants a stick in the sand and measures a shadow the length of one fiftieth of a circle. Excited, he hires a bematist to pace the span between the cities. With that information alone, he determines the size of the Earth.

Eratosthenes estimates our planet's tilt, lays an ordered grid over the whole blue sphere – the lines of latitude and longitude – and maps the known world's lands and populations. Eratosthenes invents geography.

We believe diseases are visits from evil spirits. To cure, we cast spells. Early human healing involves letting blood and boring holes in skulls. We suppose arteries carry air, and the liver holds the soul. If a man suffers burning down there, and his water's running white, like a donkey's, then the doctor boils oil, resin, vinegar, and myrrh, to pour it through a tube into his lower parts.

For thousands of years, *medicine* essentially means *imagine*.

Enter Galen, Roman physician, small in stature, meticulous taker of notes. He performs surgery on sick primates and often heals them. Instead of divination, Galen offers diagnosis. Instead of haphazard sorcery, he applies science. He observes the sinews and tissues between physical being and well-being. Galen sees how the gory mess inside us is the basis of healing – not spirits, not gods, not other worlds.

And Jesus arose from humble beginnings to an exceptional calling, preaching infinite love.

And His doctrine earned more fearers than followers.

And He was crucified among heretics and thieves, to serve as warning along the road between cities.

And three decades later, Jesus rose again without body or blood. For in the writings of Paul, Jesus was the son of the one true God, our peacemaker, redeemer, and destroyer of death.

And Paul's story inspired more poets. And their Testaments bore witness to the man-God who understood our wickedness, and who therefore returned to offer us an out: a beatific afterlife, if only we honor our neighbors, forgive others, and obey Him, the man-God, the Lord Jesus Christ.

And for three centuries, whoever obeyed Christian teachings was imprisoned and enslaved.

And so it was, until a battle for the Roman Empire, when General Constantine dreamed that Jesus was the key to victory.

And Constantine woke up to a light in the sky in the shape of a cross.

And on that day, he conquered in the name of Christ.

And on this day, Emperor Constantine calls a council to unify the Christian Church and the Roman state.

And from this date, the writings of Paul and the other poets shall be recognized as Scripture.

And within a hundred years, Christians will wield the power to undertake plundering missions, persecute other religions, and rewrite every calendar. And the rest of all our days are counted down in terms of Him.

And this shows how warlords wield faith as world force.

And this shows how poets magnified a man into a god.

Once, a flaming stone fell out of the sky. Where it crashed, the ancients dropped to their knees and bowed down, chanting, calling the sacred spot *Mecca*. They believed their heaven stone was sent from another world. And they constructed a giant cube to shelter the extraordinary thing. Thousands bowed before the cube-shaped temple with a fragment of another world inside it.

And the centuries passed.

And then a desert flood swallowed Mecca.

Now the temple must be built again. The smooth black stone that was a fire in the sky must rest upon a protective altar.

But no one's ever touched the holy relic. Who alive can bear the otherworldly honor?

Quraish tribal elders say the heaven stone must divine its own savior. Whoever wanders next over the roadway is the one.

An honest businessman passes, and stumbles into immortality. Thus elected, he moves the stone, receives a sign, and changes his name. His genius-struck soul dictates directly the voice of God (praise be unto Him).

Prophet Muhammad (peace be on him) comes to us as a mercy on the worlds, to spread the Word of the one true God (praise be unto Him). We must forget the lesser deities. We must pray, forgive, make pilgrimages, find balance, pursue chastity, fast, offer alms, and dedicate ourselves to worshipping God (praise be unto Him).

When others miss the beauty of his holy message, Muhammad (peace be on him) takes his sword and makes them listen.

Emperor Ming of Tang could absolutely get used to this. *Tick.*
Whoosh. Tick. Whoosh. A more organic, yet more mechanical,
rhythmic accompaniment for his lovemaking. *Tick. Whoosh.* Far
more congruous than the courtly players and their obsequious
flutes. This instrument's pulses even accentuate the giggles and
moans of his wives and concubines. *Tick. Whoosh.*

Well out of earshot of Ming's gross, cosmic-and-state-
regulated procreation ministrations, past the suits of armor in the
main hall of the Palace of Great Brilliance, within the main lab
of the Astronomy Department of the College of All Sages, Tang's
most esteemed star-watching mathematicians raise bronze cups
of botanical spirits to the problem-solving genius of one of their
own, the honorable I-Hsing, whose success inventing the Water-
Driven Spherical Bird's-Eye-View Map of the Heavens has
saved them from certain beheading. "To the scholar whose mind
is in tune with the Tao!" they toast.

I-Hsing's marvel may not accurately calculate the
auspicious hour for the conception of Ming's heir, but Ming's
pleasure at the mere sound of the thing is a boon to the fortitude
of his yang. And perhaps his new timepiece will also dampen
distracting conjugal asides from the empress. "Tapestries," she'd
said, in the midst of Ming's thrusts. "What the royal ceiling needs
is tapestries."

Forget them. From this day forward, Ming enjoys the
gentle tinkle of trickling waters, coupled with a periodic clacking
of jacks, punctuated by that patient, consistent bell. *Ding!* No
coitus had ever commenced so cadenced.

850 Common Era: GUNPOWDER

In Chang'an, the most populous city on the planet, Taoist alchemists meditate evenings and mornings, and conduct experiments afternoons. For a thousand years, the Tao has taught followers the Way, including techniques for achieving mmortality, which may be shown to anyone who manages to let go of worldliness and willfulness. The prefectures of the Tang Dynasty increasingly embody a debased version of Tao ideals, navigating between demonism and reason – mystic questing versus existential efforts in letting go. To reach lost souls and bring them back along the Way, a handful of elite Taoist monks, financed by the state, turn their practices to alchemy, seeking chemically what Romans called the Magnum Opus, the "philosopher's stone." They're sure there must be a vital substance – some universal element – that transforms anything into anything else, including turning mortality into eternal life.

The monastery laboratory in the geographical center of Tang accommodates a cluttered organization of glass beakers and cylinders, pipettes and flasks of viscous liquids, mortars brimming with powders and crystals, stacks of arcane tomes, rolled and unrolled scrolls, logbooks inked with symbols and theorems, snaking bamboo tubes, bones of animals, human skulls, shelves of color-coded oils, a bronze globe, hanging ornate vessels, yellow satin draperies lined with green fringe, glazed tricolored pottery, a deck of playing cards with color pictures of soldiers, a chessboard, a clay pot dripping water to mark out time, rows of tortoise shells, golden dragon head decorations, two graduated scales, a bellows, burning candles, a firepit, distillation devices, scoops, tongs, tweezers, pestles, brushes, jars, cast iron evaporation pans, and a hand-powered fan with multiple wheels to clear and condition the laboratory air. The Taoist monks who work here have accepted vows of self-abnegation, to help with which, between experiments and meditations, they sip from spirits of aloe, agaric, saffron, and gentian.

The recent obsession of the Chang'an monks is *xiao shi* – the Romans will call it *niter*, the British, *saltpeter* – because this gritty white powder features an amazingly Tao-like trait. Although xiao shi will not catch fire itself, its presence causes other matter to burn faster. Perhaps the stuff will also magnify a person's ch'i. The investigating monks of Tang have been adding it to various flammable materials.

With charcoal and sulfur, xiao shi completes a compound that flies into dancing sparks, ignites the beards of the discoverers, throws alchemists onto their backs, burns down labs, changes the Tang arrows into flying fires that will terrify invading Mongols, and travels the Silk Road to the Arab lands, where gunpowder propels heavy rounds of iron into warring Europeans who survive to render the technology central to future weaponry.

1040: ADVANCED SCIENCE

It's the Golden Age of Islam. Near the palm-lined center of a circular city in the desert with a wide moat around it, a vaulted stone library draws scholars from cultures thousands of miles distant, to study at the global hub of translation and research. In Baghdad's House of Wisdom — between walls lined with tomes, maps, and manuscripts — doctors, astronomers, translators, authors, geographers, scribes, mathematicians, and others of many genders and faiths cooperate to improve the world's technology, medicine, philosophy, and art.

Ibn al-Haytham shows us that eyes don't create what they see. Eyes interpret the contents of light.

Ibn Mūsā al-Khwārizmī derives algorithms.

Al-Jāḥiẓ designs the idea of evolution.

Sutayta al-Mahāmali develops algebra and legal theory.

Al-Kindī's numbers will forever count our quantities.

Ibn Sīnā's medical text sets standards for centuries.

Beginning by admitting their ignorance, these sages and others test beliefs, and experiment while withholding judgment. One day, when the ink of scholars runs as sacred as the blood of martyrs, we will call this mode the *scientific method*.

1215: MORE INCLUSIVE CIVIL RIGHTS

King John rules England by arbitrary brute force. His petty cruelty earns such notoriety, he inspires the Sherriff of Nottingham in the Robin Hood legend. When English barons threaten rebellion – citing health, honor, exaltation, and the ordering of the kingdom – King John relents.

Under the Catholic Church's supervision, the rebel barons draft a Magna Carta – Great Charter of Liberties. And on the banks of the Thames, beneath the flaps of an impressive makeshift pavilion, a reluctant king signs the people's demands, expanding hopeful humanity's circle of freedom.

(1) Society has a duty to serve every one of its citizens.

(2) Society must protect personal rights over property.

(3) We resent the so-called "divine right" of royalty.

(4) We resent the birth-accident of nobility.

(5) We resent unfair taxation and wealth distribution.

(6) No one, not even the highest leader, is above the law.

1327: HUMANISM

In church on Good Friday in the south of France, a poet looking up from prayer lays his eyes upon the ideal subject: Laura, whose face is *not of this earth*. She wholly possesses him, exiling the poor poet from his own wretched self. Yet he never speaks to her.

Petrarch – a name he chooses – expresses mixed feelings, enhancing his life through infinite longing. He wanders for wandering's sake, alters his identity, and becomes an emblem of rebirth, the first modern man, virtual stranger in his own skin, disenchanted, at home nowhere, writing brilliant poems that shine brighter over time. He questions every given, even God. He redefines the heart as an emotional seat where life and nature carve immortal letters. Petrarchan hearts, with two red lobes tapered to a point, forever beat, romancing our reasons for folly in love. Petrarch places happiness at the center of existence, elusive and distant, and he chases after it, yearning as he voices devoted words exposing our weird inner lives.

1350: THE PLAGUE

The warlike khans of Mongolia craved expansion and their soldiers rode without fear. For 150 years, the Golden Horde invaded, annexed, and resettled civilizations. No one could beat them, with their mounted archers and lactose tolerance. The swarming Mongol cavalry killed from distance. They drank horse milk to fight in winter. Surely, it would take an otherworldly force to offer the Mongols a worthy adversary.

Emerging from the Himalayas and migrating for a century, a mysterious plague reached Horde soldiers and lured them through fevers, chills, seizures, swollen welts, gangrenous limbs – ten days, the end.

Dwindling, desperate, plague-infected Mongols attacked at Caffa, catapulting inflicted cadavers over walls, inventing biological warfare, introducing pandemic to densely populated Europe. In the following three years, fifty million perish.

With so many workers gone, survivors' wages rise. Gift one from the plague to beleaguered humanity: labor rights.

Hospitals are converting from spirit wards – where we lie in wait for death – to science halls, where we may heal. Gift two.

The poor are buying finery – herbs, oils, furs, spices, perfumes to hide the stench of corpses – as middle classes flourish between haves and have-nots. Gift three.

With saints and priests dying alongside sinners and commoners, and no gods granting causes or cures, religion comes untied from politics. Gift four.

Instead of faith, perhaps distraction will offset suffering. Entertainment – secular fiction – elevates passive congregations into critical audiences. Gift five.

Whoever survives the plague unlocks a new genetic code. Longer life expectancy. Gift six.

The more we overcome, the more we can become. But the plague isn't some towering otherworldly enemy; it's just an ordinary bacterium, born of rat blood in the bellies of fleas.

1440: PRINTING PRESS

"Potential patrons! Curious citizens of means! You are looking at an inventor of ingenious contraptions. I'm a wizard with any material. I can synthesize magical chemicals. And with just a few of your shiny pennies, I might reshape the world!"

Johannes Gutenberg, needle-nosed grifter, chaser of get-rich-quick schemes, swindles his way into debilitating debt. He's sued by partners, pursued by creditors, and banned from his own hometown for shady dealings. Still, every new Gutenberg gem does seem promising.

He sways an investor to forget that crooked past, secures enough capital to run a farm, and what he doesn't drink away he spends on specialty machine parts and a modest workshop.

Gutenberg's latest vision combines Chinese print, Korean type, and European turnscrews and crank-handles with his proud creation – permanent, fast-drying, oil-based ink. Gutenberg assembles a machine where pressmen roll twenty sheets before a scribe copies one. Overnight, publishing becomes the first mechanized industry.

Gutenberg's investor realizes the value, steals his work, and garners the praise. Gutenberg himself dies penniless. But his printing and stamping, with no driving of the pen, brings information to any literate person. Without effort and without glasses, anyone may read, which diminishes reliance on distant elites. The printing press raises our voices, shifts power toward the many, and spreads humanity's ultimate resource: knowledge.

1444: TARGETED ENSLAVEMENT

There's a new small castle by the coastline in west central Africa with a makeshift wharf attached. The white men came from Portugal in the north and built all of it in a year. The soldiers who guard the place have matchlock guns. No one else has guns. Those soldiers offer money to any who'll kidnap other people and bring them to their new small castle on the African coast.

Many brutal men are chasing that money, roaming the countryside, seeking innocent villagers. They hear laughing children playing hide-and-seek in the woods and they catch them and gag them and take them to holding pens. They find a young woman at the riverbank collecting water, thinking about her lover and the tryst they'd just shared, and sneaking up they capture her and carry her to the filthy pens. Seizing a grown man alive is difficult, but also more valuable, and the ruthless slavers manage it with planning and some luck, even if the man they target has many close friends. And then with their bounties of stolen souls chained together – people whose joys and dreams have been destroyed, whose lives and families are left behind, whose individual stories will be lost to history – the bands of slavers march to reach the new small castle on the African coast, where the people they've kidnapped are packed into ships, laid side by side, shackled in the holds, branded, and carried months at sea, to be sold to high bidders and overworked on dangerous plantations. Most who make it that far will die within two years.

An unfree workforce of debtors, criminals, foreigners, infidels, and captives of war has always driven civilized progress. But as Portugal uses guns and money to pick and choose who'll be enslaved, an even more inhumane foundation is laid for the future of the human. What begins as commerce in the bodies of Black people soon becomes the commerce of the world.

1450: CAPITALISM

Off the coast of Morocco, Portuguese sailors discover an ideal land for sugar creation: a mountainous, uninhabited island so forest-filled they name it *Madeira*, their word for wood. Within thirty years, Portugal's enslaved African laborers clear the Madeiran woodland and plant green canes from shore to shore.

Human bodies require and digest many ingredients, but the only fare that feeds our brains is sugar. Our metabolism turns other foods into it. We're built to crave the sweet stuff. But sugar crops require tending and watering under hot sun, rushed harvesting, and processing in dangerous boiling houses. Machete carriers work alongside mill feeders, prepared to lop off arms in case hands get caught. Scalding sugar sticks to skin like glue, eating into muscle before it cools.

Because no person should be forced to work on sugar plantations, Europeans decide a slave counts less than a person. And because the fuelwood of Madeira won't sustain sugar refinement, Europeans sail to seek more sugar islands. Soon their Age of Discovery will find them pillaging the Americas.

On Madeira, Portugal conceives of humankind's enduring global system: capitalism. From Madeira, we set the new course for existence, chasing commodity frontiers, using unfree people to clear a land, no matter who lives there, reseed a land, no matter what grew there, strip a land for all that it's worth, and then move on.

1522: CIRCUMNAVIGATION

Enrique, a boy born in the heart of the so-called Spice Islands, goes fishing one morning, gets kidnapped by pirates, and ends up in Malaysia, where he's sold into slavery to Ferdinand Magellan, a Portuguese ship captain, who's taken with young Enrique's cunning attitude and his language expertise. Magellan employs the lad as an interpreter, and brings him to Europe, where seafaring superpowers Spain and Portugal vie in the first space race to see who can claim more global territory and source more sugar and spice.

Magellan, with Enrique by his side, proposes to Spain that he can sail west and find the Spice Islands, a feat that would prove what Pythagoras proposed two millennia before: the Earth is round. And soon, four carracks and one caravel leave from Spanish waters to sail around the back of the world under Magellan's command.

The armada winters in South America for three months, where unrest grows. The men fear endless storms, impenetrable fog, whirlpools, icebergs, Indigenous warriors, leviathans, mermaids, centaurs, eagles so large they could carry the men from the decks, and, most of all, the great unknown. Magellan cajoles them with promises: familiar stars, calm waters, and guiding angels strumming soothing harps. He also threatens them with brute force. But the Spanish sailors feel no loyalty to a Portuguese ship captain.

Enrique's unfazed by months at sea, untroubled by the mythical fears of white men. And as for their feelings about their captain – Magellan's will bequeaths that when he dies, Enrique may breathe free.

When the men mutiny, one boat is lost, another returns home, and many sailors are quartered, beheaded, and their bodies displayed to dissuade future subversion.

Magellan, Enrique, and three vessels continue on, and the fated expedition discovers stormy southern straits connecting east and west. Past treacherous waters, the crews become the first Europeans to sail the Pacific Ocean.

And sail the Pacific Ocean. And sail the Pacific Ocean.

Food spoils. Scurvy strikes. There's mass starvation. It's a hundred days before the troubled seamen touch land at Guam, where they slaughter many locals and burn down many houses.

A month later, Enrique reaches his homeland among the Spice Islands, where Magellan dies in a skirmish. But the rest of the sea dogs refuse to honor the will that says Enrique may breathe free. Undaunted, he schemes, and his people riddle Magellan's men with arrows during a farewell dinner.

At last, Enrique the free man, after twelve long years, settles in among his family and grows old as the first person to circumnavigate the globe.

1543: HELIOCENTRISM

Town gossips risk prison on blasphemy charges even whispering the breaking news. *The Church is really wrong this time.* A scientist has insulted Scripture, again. But this time, the math and observations carry proof.

Fearing holy wrath, Nicolaus Copernicus has waited to disclose the sacrilege from his deathbed. He disputes not only core beliefs, but also common sense.

The Earth revolves around the Sun.

If holy teaching can be wrong – if "facts" we learn from heaven can be proven wrong – it's the dawn of a new paradigm.

By revising light, Copernicus shows us we aren't the focus of the universe. Night is nothing but our planet's shadow lifting as we turn to face the morning.

The Earth revolves around the Sun.

1597: ENGINEERING

As the seventeenth century approaches, most of Europe grows affluent by pillaging the rest of the world, stripping foreign lands of their resources, enslaving, subjugating, and indenturing populations for cheap labor. The wealth of this enormous theft creates a European middle class with schooling and time to devote to innovation.

William Shakespeare is enchanting language, Giordano Bruno is expanding outer space, the world's calendar is being catholically fixed, and the new sorcery – science – is breaking faith and selling out. "Knowledge itself is power," Francis Bacon writes. And businesses begin funding scientists.

Engineers transform the problems of the world into paddlewheels, piledrivers, coil springs, floating docks, grenade muskets, centrifugal pumps, countless handy gadgets. We don't seek truth anymore from our scientific sorcerers. Modern Europeans prefer useful toys.

1600: CORPORATIONS

A group of London merchants signs a contract so far-reaching they conceive a bodiless being who straddles the globe. By royal charter, on this final day of the year of our Lord 1600, Queen Elizabeth the First of England signs into existence an actual superhuman – a multinational corporation – the Governor and Company of Merchants of London Trading into the East Indies.

The East India Company, or EIC, as the virtual avatar is known, sends tall ships packed with wool, metals, and silver bullion from Leadenhall Docks to stops along the new Silk and Spice Roads, paved with blue ocean. They trade for cotton, saltpeter, porcelain, opium. The EIC defines its own purpose, controls commerce free of scrutiny, recruits an army and a navy, and reaps profit without responsibility, more like a country than a company. For centuries, the EIC not only corners trade, but wins wars, absorbs land, and creates colonies. A board of directors rules a fifth of the world's population.

Businessmen update the bottom line of our destiny. By an invisible hand, toward progress and devastation, the fewer and fewer steer the many.

1604: MICROSCOPES AND TELESCOPES

Because eyes, miraculous as they are, developed for half a billion years within the light-inflecting viscosity of oceans, the thin air's unfiltered glare has rendered human eyes imperfect instruments. We strain our ciliary muscles squinting far and near.

To see, it seems we've always had glasses perched on our noses, but no one remembers them landing there. At least since pictograms refined into letters, monks and scribes have peered through curved glass shards to magnify manuscripts. By 1300, spectacles were common in Europe. By 1400, symmetrical bent lenses, mounted and framed, signaled intelligence.

This whole time, half-blind humankind stares past a discovery no one imagines until a Dutch youngster at play in a glass shop refocuses us. Through two overlapping lenses, a cork's holes swell to the size of caves, and a faraway barn appears close enough to punch.

Forget eyeglasses. With spyglasses, we gaze from atoms to galaxies.

1610: ASTRONOMY

Through his "perspective glass," a natural philosopher peers into heaven's corners and confirms the Church's fears. The fixed stars are flaming suns, perhaps with wandering bodies like Earth encircling them.

Galileo Galilei records the phases of Venus, counts four satellites orbiting Jupiter, and runs his magnified eyes over the rough face of the Moon. No one else has looked at light that takes as long to reach here. No one else has seen so far back in time.

The father of observation brings us further into focus. Galileo witnesses the heavenly firmament as anything but firm.

1644: FREEDOM OF THE PRESS

In Britain, no book, pamphlet, or paper shall be printed unless approved and licensed by the state.

It's not consensus, it's a decree.

John Milton, respected poet and civil servant, takes exception to the censor's rule. Censorship, he says, disexercises and blunts abilities, and hinders and crops discovery. Books contain a potency of life to be as active as their author, whose children they become. To kill a good book is to kill a soul, to massacre the breath of reason, to slay immortality.

According to Milton, humans develop by circulating ideas. Who's a worthy editor to blot and alter hidebound humors? We must feel free to set forth in public for whatever purpose, even to admonish the state.

Milton, perhaps the last person to pore through every existing publication, reads himself blind, writes a stunning liturgical poem, coins six hundred words — *stunning, liturgical, disexercises, earthshaking, lovelorn, terrific, pandemonium, fragrance* — and eloquently declares that power must never silence people.

1666: MODERN CITIES

Great fire is coming! For seventeen years – since King Charles I's beheading ended the English Civil War – Puritans in London have foretold a fate for their country's immoral behavior. *Great fire is coming!*

Puritan gospel turns prophecy Sunday morning as a Pudding Lane bakery ignites. By dusk, the London skyline shimmers under a ceiling of hellish smoke.

Monday dawns on three hundred buildings burning. Londoners form lines in bucket brigades, then end up scattering, burying mementos in hiding spots. Hundreds of thousands escape on rickety carts, though there's nowhere to go.

Tuesday, strong winds fan the high flames higher. Many fear that all of London will be lost.

Wednesday, Charles II orders a perimeter of buildings destroyed by gunpowder blasts. Destruction meets destruction, and the Great Fire of London flickers down, contained. Most of the city, erased. More than thirteen thousand houses, gone. Reports are saying nine dead, but the tallies don't include the poor.

The Dutch and French are blamed. Everyone thinks it was arson. Charles II condemns the hand of God, and Puritans act righteous. British courts convict and execute a Frenchman, though he wasn't in London when the conflagration began. Later, the incident's proven an accident – the fault of stray oven sparks drifting onto canvas flour sacks.

London's reconstruction takes two decades and reinvents how we live together in groups, with zoning for gardens and parks, wider alleys and streets, hydrant systems, insurance companies, real estate markets, neighborhoods, downtowns, slums. Welcome to the metropolis. If you can afford it.

1687: CALCULATION

Hundreds of miles from each other, two European mathematicians huddle over candlelit writing desks for months, trying to rationalize irrational problem-solving. Each one's independent reckonings of complex equations arrive at similar interpretations of what seems like a master code.

The calculus.

Gottfried Leibniz, the last universal genius, and Isaac Newton, who sees an apple falling and understands gravity, both wield numbers and symbols to verify that science is more powerful than sorcery. In their work, wild fictions translate to fast facts. Their system of computation proves so abstract, it does away with objects in the world, figuring everything as formulas. *Differentials*, Leibniz calls them. *The method of fluxions and fluents*, writes Newton. A point is indivisible. A line has many points. A surface, many lines. A volume, many surfaces. Calculus articulates the limits and the changes. With the calculus, we trace a missing sense behind nature's mysteriousness.

1712: INDUSTRIALIZATION

The timber in Europe's almost all felled. Larch, pine, spruce, hornbeam – clear-cut and built with, chopped down and burned. Houses from London to Munich go cold.

An answer lies under the ground. They call it *coal*. They say it's like denser fire. All we have to do is find it, dig it, haul it, burn it, and channel carbonic energy.

Here is a mine containing the coal that'll warm the rich citizens of Europe.

Here are the miners who'll dig in the dark and blacken their lungs or die in cave-ins to carve out the mine containing the coal that'll warm the rich citizens of Europe.

Here's a machine that transforms steam. It pumps out the water that fills in the mine to help out the miners who dig up the coal that'll warm the rich citizens of Europe.

Harnessing steam, we turn heat into motion, engineering industry's revolution. Ready or not, we're masters of energy conversion: coal, oil, electricity, magnetism, the atom.

Here is the line to assemble machines that assemble machines to assemble machines, so people work less and their products increase, exploiting the Earth as our world revolves and revolves and evolves around industry.

1796: VACCINATION

A silent, speckled monster wiped out Incans and Aztecs. Invisible until it eats, the pestilent brute played a part in ending the Roman Empire. By 1700, half a million "top predator" humans succumbed yearly to the ethereal creature. Now, as the nineteenth century approaches, all over the world, those who aren't slain are stained – scarred, blinded, disfigured – which means they're also spared if the pox-bringing assassin comes for them again.

Smallpox shares its food of flesh with an ugly but benign pox-twin who visits cows but never kills. That other pox's boils pass from dairy udders to milkmaids' hands. Cowpox-infected maids feel fine applying salves and creams. In public, they wear elegant gloves. In experiments, they show resistance to smallpox.

A natural scientist from England pits one pox-bringer against another. Edward Jenner thinks our bodies can be taught to beat diseases. Sure enough, he extracts the matter from a cowpox lesion, injects it into a youngster's arm, and notes how the boy's system, exposed to smallpox, has grown immune.

For a long time, we thought lightning was the sky attacking us. Then those flashes gave us fire. Soon we felt the bursts came from the gods. Lately, lightning's considered an imponderable fluid running into or throughout reality, something akin to gravity.

Natural philosophers hazard jolts to conduct experiments. What exactly is the power that leaps from heaven and flicks between our fingers in sharp sparks? Is it a series of quick vibrations? Some sort of energy progression? Is electricity just one thing? Or do two entities grind against each other and generate moments of thrilling results?

By 1750, we suspected two separate electricities existed. We produced them by friction. Both kinds could be stored. They'd jolt with ease from place to place, even between bodies.

In 1752, kite-flying Benjamin Franklin watched bolts from the clouds flit among conditions of excess and deficiency. He named the conditions *charges*, and demonstrated only one electricity switched between positive and negative charges.

In the 1780s, Luigi Galvani animated dead frogs with live current. Galvani figured lightning was organic. But Alessandro Volta disagreed. To prove this awesome force wasn't a property of bodily tissue, Volta spent a decade trying to electrify metallic conductors.

Volta introduces water, in the form of moistened cardboard strips laced between zinc and copper disks. He stacks the wet couplings, wires them, and the inorganic, ungainly pile charges and never discharges. It maintains a steady state. A voltage. A seemingly endless circulation of electric . . . who knows?

1814: ASTROPHYSICS

At war with Napoleon, the Kingdom of Bavaria turns to technology. The Optical Institute in Munich hires a master in the art of melting, stirring, blowing, cutting, grinding, pressing, smoothing, and polishing optical glass. Joseph von Fraunhofer gains top security clearance to explore the possibilities of aiming, range-finding, and reconnaissance. Working in a dream laboratory, Fraunhofer refines perhaps the purest surface the universe has ever seen through, to refocus implausible distances.

In the Wars of Liberation, against the French, his field instruments lend coalition generals tactical advantages.

Fraunhofer also likes to play with prisms. Fascinated by sunshine's colorful dispersal, he studies prismatic rays through telescopes, and catches tiny distinctions among the tinges. He doesn't know it, but the patterned lines he sees are shadows cast by atoms.

Fraunhofer hand-copies the banded designs, unwittingly forging signatures for a dozen elements, tracing the fingerprints of the heavens. His precise notations of thick and thin strokes show the chemical composition of the Sun.

Napoleon Bonaparte surrenders, and Joseph von Fraunhofer's appointed a title in the Order of Merit. But more importantly and surprisingly, Fraunhofer becomes the accidental father of the "new astronomy."

His spectral lines spell the letters of a language that will teach us our address in the universe. It's a language that tells us what we're made of. It's a language that says we're insignificant.

1821: MOTORS

As the nineteenth century began, the battery was born. We raised a little lightning, even if we didn't know what it was. And in the two decades since, no one's figured out what to make lightning do. Our scant imagination reduces the bringer of fire to a sideshow dancer, as wealthy socialites pay well to squint at flashes and static lifting the hair of a shocked volunteer.

After twenty confused years, a young man who has risen from poverty makes the case that electricity can steer the world. He catches the attention of an eminent scientist, and starts an apprenticeship that earns him access to his own basement lab. On Christmas morning, he tinkers together an "apparatus for revolution of wire and magnet," and dangles a bit of copper into a cup of liquid mercury, all connected to a weak battery. With no physical contact and no apparent effort, around and around the charged wire spins. He calls his brother-in-law George over to witness. "Do you see, do you see, do you see, George?"

Everyone soon sees that a poor, uneducated genius has converted electricity into mechanical energy. Michael Faraday has invented the motor. And motors will speed us past limits.

By wand or wish, by spirit or trust, by luck or fantastic technology, we've enhanced ourselves with once inconceivable superpowers. Our species is fed, protected, and accommodated like no species ever before. Tools, music, images, languages, stories, maths, monies, machines transform us into different kinds of beings from what we might have been. No matter our motives, we're devising new ways to do unlikely things we never could have known we wanted done.

Nicéphore Niépce, gentleman of science, is already father to a pair of superhuman enhancers – the internal combustion engine and the bicycle – but when he pursues his dream of becoming an artist, Niépce possesses no skill with palette or paint. So he does what any gentleman of science might do: he tries to trick the Sun into decorating his canvases for him.

To sketch with daylight's gestures, Niépce invents sensitive varnishes and sets out stencils over lithographic stones. Nine years pass without progress as he mixes chemicals and experiments. Then he follows an ancient hint from Arab polymath Ibn al-Haytham. Niépce cuts a small hole in the window shutters of his dark upstairs work chamber to project a beam of light across the room. Opposite the shutters, upon his wall, the focused light throws a page-sized, inverted portrait of what's outside: a barn roof, a pear tree, a pigeon house, the sky.

Niépce hangs a pewter plate coated with asphalt, exposing it for hours to the flipped image his camera obscura reveals. As dusk falls, by the glow of a chimney lamp, he washes the plate with lavender oil and petroleum jelly. Asphalt holds solid in the brightest spots and rinses from shadowy places. A scientist has fixed what mirrors reflect without the aid of a painter's brush. There, upon the plate, exposed, ghostly and faint, smelling wonderful: a barn roof, a pear tree, a pigeon house, the sky. It's the first picture taken by the Sun.

1831: ELECTROMAGNETISM

Ten years ago, the rich started running on electricity. Their scary weird force grants more motion and strength. Machines lift twenty times their own weight. Wealthy white men form companies to control the fluency of power's resistance and potential.

Michael Faraday caused this craze, but he isn't interested in energy's uses. He wants to understand electricity's source. Faraday feels from his nerves to his bones how magnets might work as motivators.

Once an amateur, now laboratory director at London's Royal Institution, Faraday has access to fine equipment and materials. He fashions an apparatus with an iron ring, wound around by copper coils, and then charges the ungainly thing with a battery of metallic plates. Over weeks, he builds to one hundred plate-pairs – an absurd concentration of potency – without progress.

They say Faraday's insane, at least misguided. There's no basis for connecting magnetic draw and electric flow. What the mad scientist proposes would bring power on demand. Impossible.

Faraday thinks. An almost divine idea strikes. The pieces of his new electrical machine must be kept in motion.

Sure enough, the next experiment brings success. Faraday's trembling dynamo demonstrates a fusing of forces. His scientific witchcraft reduces everything to fields and vibrations. Electromagnetism induces live current from thin air.

Soon, this mad science will cook our food, heat and cool houses, display ideal realities, and bathe us all in constant light.

1837: TELECOMMUNICATIONS

Ever since we could speak, we've tried to be heard from far away. To throw our voices, we've learned to pass notes: glints of sunlight off chips of glass, puff of smoke, trained pigeon, flashing beacon, waving flag, horseback, steamship, locomotive . . .

It's the 1830s. We're in charge of ingenious machinery. Our superpowered engines drive on leashes of coal and electricity. Even still, it takes a year for messages to circumnavigate the globe.

Many scientists, engineers, and businessmen cooperate, incorporate, compete, secure funding, litigate, build up networks of information-sharing innovation, and boast quite loudly. Famine rages in Ireland, Indigenous families across the United States are being forced from their homes, and British soldiers are murdering Aboriginal people in Australia by the millions. But instead of raising money and using machines to solve these evils, the rich are talking about talking.

Over sending sources of electricity, through insulated lines to receiving indicators and back, along Earth-return circuits – electromagnetism delivers distant words instantly.

Samuel Morse's taps in Washington beep in Baltimore STOP He wonders aloud what God has wrought STOP World shrinks as economy expands STOP We can whisper everywhere at once STOP But what are we saying STOP .-- . / -.-. .- -. / .-- ....--. ... .-. / ... .- .-. .-. --. --. .... .- . / .-- / --- -. .-.-. / ... .- --- .-- . / -.... .- - / .-- .... .- - / .- .-. . / .-- . / .... .- -.-- .. -. --. / ... .- --- .--.

1838: MECHANICAL CALCULATION

Countess Ada Byron, Lady Lovelace, opens the door to her sensible London flat. "Charles! Whatever is the matter?"

Standing there, sweating and exasperated, is her work partner and fellow scientist, the esteemed Charles Babbage.

"He has demanded more money!" Babbage agitates as he enters. "And the salon in five days!"

"There, there." Lovelace touches his arm, leading the heavy-breathing man to her green divan across the sunny room.

"Clement said I ordered a first-rate article, and as such I must be content to pay more for him to deliver it."

"Dear, dear," answers the countess, patting Babbage on the arm. "And what about the public coffers?"

"There's no time to grovel before treasury cads! It takes those fools a week to lift a pen and drag it on a scrap of paper."

Lovelace wags her fantastic purple hat. "Don't worry, Charles. You shall pay dear Clement this very afternoon."

"But, Ada!"

She laughs. "I live within my means, Mr. Babbage. And although we've toiled together these many years, you've never asked me for a penny of my family's money. On Saturday, the world must see the benefit of your great work."

"*Our* great work, Ada," Babbage corrects, squeezing her hand. "You understand the Difference Engine better than I do."

Lovelace and Babbage's Difference Engine is the size of a schoolroom, uses eight thousand parts, weighs five tons, and will never be fully built. Only an intricate fragment ever clicks, spins, and eliminates human error from numerical calculation.

On Saturday night in the drawing room of a flat where Dorset Street runs into Manchester, British socialites from Darwin to Dickens watch as Babbage's white-gloved hand turns a brass crank and sets in motion cams, gears, levers, rods, springs, precisely aligned number wheels, and the future of computers.

1839: SOLAR ENERGY

At this address – Planet Earth, Inner Solar System, Orion Arm of the Milky Way, Laniakea Supercluster, the Known Universe – we're alive because a dedicated star showers us in constant energy. Every erg, amp, watt, volt, and joule on Earth emerged as solar power first. Every step. Every thought. When hungry lions gnaw the entrails of fresh-killed gazelles, they're chewing recycled sunshine. Eat a carrot, the calories in it started out as daylight. This very second, our celestial host produced enough juice to run every machine here for a year – if only we could zap that light right to electricity.

In Paris, Edmond Becquerel, a talented, privileged teenager experimenting with batteries he builds in his dad's lab, measures how much current shifts when clumpy red powder – selenium – touches Sun. Becquerel unveils the photovoltaic effect: how light might become directly electric.

It'll take us two centuries to photosynthesize efficiently. At our address, residents invest in local fuels instead of a star.

Charles Darwin sails the world, studies nature, collects samples, conducts experiments, and interprets data. He observes how teeth sprout from the jaws of prenatal whales. How fossils tell us gills in ancient fish turned into inner ears. How snake embryos bear token leg bumps. How bird beaks align with bird diets – short and thick to crush a seed, or long and thin to suck at nectar.

Darwin wonders. If, as the Church relates, God's perfect world is complete and unchanging, then what of this evidence to the contrary? If God created flawless creatures, then why are we developing?

With each impression penciled in his leather journals, Darwin knows he risks imprisonment. *Surely two distinct creators must have been at work.* He fears he's abetting a murder, where the victim is God, and the killer was the co-creator, nature. *Descent with modification*, he writes. It's scientific code for blasphemy.

Darwin's riotous words insult sensibilities, including his own. He doesn't publish until a fellow naturalist, Alfred Russel Wallace, arrives at the same conclusions. It seems a human is just another animal with more favorable adaptations.

1842: MATERIALISM

We yearn for certainty, but our searches over thousands of generations have offered scarce assurances. We'll never know the gods, the Sun always rises then sets, the seasons cycle through changes, and everybody dies. In our vulnerable condition, we've grown wise enough to learn the tales in Nature's book, but rash enough to rewrite how the story ought to go. Brave, reckless, we read ahead – intending to edit life in our favor.

Four organic physics doctoral students at the University of Berlin coordinate a study across multiple fields, and they swear that they've discovered a scientific certainty. Their rationale challenges belief, but they have enough data to prove it: no other powers exist beyond the physical. Love, anger, fire, steam, electricity, ice, happiness, freethinking – everything – reduces to the stillness and motions of material particles.

At the inaugural meeting of their natural science club, Brücke, Reymond, Helmholtz, and Ludwig sign and seal an oath in their own blood. They swear we're nothing more than matter. There's no such thing as life force. There's no such thing as God.

1846: SOAP

Fish flash their scales against corals and rocks. Cats often lick their various parts. Ground squirrels roll in pungent dirt. Bees preen their wings on airflow, in flight. Sparrows flutter in dry dust or pools of water. Pigs strut, seeming fresher, whenever they muddy their coats. Hippos wallow. Horses groom. Primates pick and brush and clean.

Filthy humans drowned the reeks of early towns in crude perfumes. The Indus rinsed in milk and rosewater. Babylonians bathed with ash and boiled fat. By 1600 BCE, Egyptians cleansed their skins in salty oils. A thousand years later, Phoenicians convened in plastered rooms to lather goat tallow. Early Romans soaked in running water, scrubbing with urine. Medieval Celts smeared themselves with sheep grease. Early modern Brits dipped in tubs of mud and dung. Renaissance Christians seldom ever sponged – it's just too sensual. Others doused in coconut oil and soil and scoured each other. The rich in many places spruced themselves under sudsy water.

In a Viennese clinic, a surgeon rubs his hands and instruments with diluted chlorine, and his patients stop contracting post-op fever. Disease is thought to spread by seed, cloud, vapor, witchcraft, spiritual demeanor, evil wishes, imbalanced humors, rank odors. But after Ignaz Semmelweis sterilizes against bacteria, global life expectancy rises steeply. We see diseases can be simply washed away.

1848: COMMUNISM

Two philosophers publish the terms to liberate society and provide equal opportunity. They've hit at the root of suffering, and that root is money.

Their manifesto contends that greed has stolen creative essence from our species. To correct the sad effects of industry, we must abolish private property, eliminate country and nationality, eradicate family inheritance, and establish level fields among workers, women, and men. We must seek this greater good by any means necessary.

Within a hundred years of these strident words, half the planet's regimes will have risen up inspired by them.

But the philosophers misjudge the aspirations of the masses — how readily we'd trade creativity for comfort; how we prefer higher authorities to guide us; how we'd rather play on teams, even if our teams exploit us; how we seem to love to be drugged to sleep. Perhaps our real species essence is obedience.

The philosophers also misjudge the selfishness of elites. Wherever a communist revolution occurs, a fascist dictator seizes control, equalizing communities under yoke and mandate, an ironic perversion of impartial utopia. Perhaps our real species essence is dominance.

Karl Marx and Friedrich Engels reinterpret the world to aid the many, but their ideas are twisted by a powerful few.

1867: WOMEN VOTING

Since the birth of democracy, votes have counted as the great societal equalizer. Votes have also been restricted on the basis of religion, race, class, gender, age, criminal past, and residency. In almost all democracies throughout history, private property has enjoyed more voting clout than actual people. Our best chance at just governance is having a say in who governs us, which might explain why unjust governors fear giving everyone a say.

The first time a woman votes in a federal election, on an island called Man, her suffrage does little to advance the social plights of her gender. Lily Maxwell's ballot grants no women access to land, learning, work, fair wages, bodily autonomy, or freedom from sexual violence, but her presence at the polls does stir a primal masculine dread. Perhaps men fear a future where the women understand how much they really don't need men.

1877: SOUND RECORDING

A brash, optimistic New Jerseyan with an urge for world change inspires a monopoly – Western Union Telegraph Company – to dedicate funds to his ingenuity. Thomas Edison spends their seed money to invent an invention factory – a workshop for creating the new. His goal is to build what everyone wants, at prices anyone can pay. Edison promises minor innovations every ten days and earth-shattering ones twice a year. Ignoring drought, mass starvation, economic depression, and a rash of industrial accidents, he focuses instead on improving communication.

Months later, experimenting, the opportunistic Edison yells across a tightened parchment attached to a needle on a Morse transmitter. He hopes his yell will force the needle to prick his finger. It does!

He lays a foil beneath the fine point and yells again, then considers the rough track that it scratches. The indentation is distinctive, and the foil holds its shape. As he passes the needle back over the groove, vibrations shiver the parchment.

Enthusiastic, Edison fashions a cylinder encircled by foil that touches a needle attached to a diaphragm. While reeling the device, he calls the first words he thinks. And then, re-reeling, he hears his calls repeat, *Mary had a little lamb*, as if spoken by a ghost.

1879: LIGHT BULBS

In the two years since Edison immortalized voices and became a household name, his invention factory has expanded to include a carpenter shed, a forge, a library, a hot glass shop, and a shack for harvesting lampblack from the chimneys of a hundred ever-burning kerosene lamps. Nothing to solve the world's mounting troubles, but plenty to enhance the leisure of the relatively rich. Machinists, technicians, chemists, mathematicians, carpenters, glassblowers, and metallurgists arrive from globe-wide to join Edison's team and play with his innovative insights and designs.

Their main workspace, surrounded by high windows, accommodates a cluttered organization of microscopes, spectroscopes, telephones, phonographs, rubber belts, galvanic batteries, shelves of capped bottles brimming with many-colored powders and liquids, glass cases of machine-part models and molds, a ten-horsepower steam engine, various needles, plugs, wires, pens, papers, tubes, cylinders, lamps, plates, foils, rings, gears, gaskets, cranks, wheels, circuits, fuses, capacitors, transmitters, a dog-eared copy of the complete poems of Edgar Allan Poe, and a *Sacred Songs and Solos* opened to the rousing tune "The Great Physician" upon the music stand of a magnificent pipe organ.

This week, the great physician of New Jersey is considering the Holy Grail of technical problems – how to produce light from electricity. Even the stock market pays attention, as investors place bets on Edison's flop or success.

A vacuum-sealed bulb seems ideal for housing brilliance. But no one knows how to close the circuit inside it. Every filament that flares up, burns out.

Then Edison has an idea so bright it becomes the symbol for having an idea. A single carbonized cotton strand, lighted at midnight, glows inside its bulb till well past noon the next day.

Newspapers announce, *Success in a Cotton Thread!* And from now on, we'll always be able to see in the dark.

1886: AUTOMOBILES

Four wheels, two axles, one carriage, an engine, a fuel tank, a steering stick – and Karl Benz invents the gas-driven car. A trip that lasted days now takes under an hour. Not since we climbed down from trees have we overseen so much horizon.

    We used to haunt the same hometowns our whole lives. Today, our feet are rubber tires, and motor wagons modify us into panting centaurs galloping high speeds for miles without stopping. And soon our toxic breath shall choke the Earth.

1895: MOTION PICTURES

Action! A pumping steam train glides into the faces of alarmed Parisians, and no audience will ever see itself the same way again. Stories and images have always spoken to imaginations, but they always had imaginations speaking back. Then the Lumières – two brothers whose name means *light* – run film stock through flickering light boxes aimed at screens in darkened rooms, setting realistic pictures in motion. Now we can all sit still, relax, and have our imaginations spoken for. *Cut!*

1900: QUANTUM MECHANICS

It's either the Gay Nineties or the *fin de siècle*. A momentous beginning or a dying close.

After centuries of progress, we think we've got the whole world figured out. The gloved and goggled rich can zip around in autos, posing for pictures. Popular culture is all the rage.

At the same time, from other angles, our prognosis isn't good. Three-quarters of us live in poverty. Every corner of the planet's been explored – but also exploited. Many mysteries have been revealed – yet nothing's taught us who we are or why we're here. Science, science fiction, philosophy, poetry, religion, all seem unified, each proclaiming everything's a sign – but the signs all say we're approaching the End of Days.

In such a climate, a physics professor researches heat. Max Planck sees heat increasing material frequencies, glowing red then yellow then white. But against predictions, the energy of heat isn't equal across its frequencies. Planck surmises, then proves, how energy travels in packets, called *quanta*. His math shows quanta acting stranger than the universe they quantify.

A new science – quantum physics – studies implications.

Here in our world of space and light, between the stones and stars, we observe a certain set of universal laws. But, also from here, the fundamental particles seem founded on illusions. Within an atom, something chaotic revises the script.

It's a spiritual and material awakening, with numerical backing. Science shows we're formed of vibrating energy signatures. It's not the End of Days if we're made of possibilities.

1903: POWERED FLIGHT

We've arrived at the edge of the nest, prepared to be pushed, ready to turn into birds or die trying.

Math can calculate balance and lift. Internal combustion harnesses power. Are we stupid or smart enough to actually fly?

Wilbur and Orville Wright convert their bike shop into an aeronautical laboratory and place a bet which one will be the first to soar. The brothers build an engine, special steering, and fixed wings to carry them, and then to carry us all.

On December 17, the Wright boys toss a coin and Orville flies first – then Wilbur, then Orville again – up and down along the seaside dunes of Kill Devil Hills, North Carolina.

A telegram to their father reads *Success four flights Thursday morning all against twenty-one mile wind started from level with engine power alone average speed through air thirty-one miles longest fifty-seven seconds inform press home Christmas* and the sky is no longer a ceiling.

1905: RELATIVITY

A boy who wouldn't allow himself to be told anything becomes a man who alters the course of everything. Working as a clerk in Switzerland after dropping out of school, he mindlessly stamps patents for colder refrigerators and more accurate clocks. But he's also a math prodigy whose mind extends as he daydreams the properties of matter, time, and light.

What if light is flexible? What if energy and mass are interchangeable? What if time is physical? The word atom *means indivisible, but an alien world spins inside an atom. Within that world, what can we measure?*

The clerk seeks numerical proofs for his baffling questions. And when he solves them, his name becomes a synonym for genius. Albert Einstein.

The quintessential mad scientist, with wild hair and luminous eyes, champion of creative nonconformity, Einstein redefines space-time entanglements. Leaping counterintuitively with imaginative math, he releases minute particles into vast energies. He pioneers a science that leads to lasers, solar panels, automatic doors, night vision, burglar alarms, the Internet, GPS navigation, weather forecasting, atomic bombs.

The fundamental mechanics that Einstein discovers prove maddeningly relative. His math shows we live in a cosmos without cause.

1907: PLASTICS

Leo Baekeland got rich in Belgium inventing better photographic paper. Now proudly American, the image of the prosperous immigrant businessman, Baekeland focuses on electrochemistry. He's a genius at molecular synthesis, and he knows how to follow the money.

Hired to insulate electric wire, Baekeland turns for inspiration to natural plastics, such as amber from sap, and shellac excreted by lac bugs. He experiments with resins, seeking something malleable and insoluble that never softens.

Baekeland submits phenol and formaldehyde to elevated temperatures and pressures, and succeeds in creating a glistening foam that can be molded completely, will harden instantly, and then becomes almost impervious to change. He names the first synthetic plastic Bakelite, after himself.

Appliances, toys, clothes, medical equipment, building materials, packaging, signs – the utility of plastic seems infinite. And soon the stuff shall coat the Earth.

1908: NITROGEN SYNTHESIS

The planet teems with a godlike being who hacks into systems. Humans have learned to mingle, heat, and pressure elemental materials. Previously, only stars performed such alchemy.

After German industrial chemists successfully synthesize nitrogen, a vital ingredient for sustaining life, artificial fertilizer helps feed billions.

Meanwhile, the German state and other states are weaponizing this vital ingredient for causing mass death. Nitrate-rich explosives power the Great War, killing millions.

We work the Earth till it behaves like a junior star, and humankind multiplies. Yet the process consumes our humanity with the power to destroy.

1927: UNCERTAINTY PRINCIPLE

As the 1920s began to roar for the quarter of us who could afford to join the roaring, a German physicist researched the realm inside atoms – quantum space – and wrote a brief scholarly paper. His numbers proved that nothing is definite, observation affects reality, and we must hold beliefs if we're to understand.

Five years later, Werner Heisenberg's pamphlet wins him the Nobel Prize. In effect, his math resurrects the Almighty as a unifying scientific principle. Our future god is fashioned in our image, and Uncertainty is its name.

1928: ANTIBIOTICS

Human bodies are only partly human. Among our cells, trillions of autonomous creatures have colonized. Microbial guests swim on us and in us, friendly, unnoticed, but their presence can also turn poison. Infection is often fatal.

Until a London lab technician finds an equipment contamination that intrigues him: within the ruined samples in his petri dishes, underneath a microscope, Alexander Fleming sees a spongy golden mold attacking tiny puffs of bacteria. He collects the slime and steeps a grotesque concoction that bolsters bodily defenses.

Penicillin kills many small organisms to protect a big one. What was terminal to us is now just a nuisance.

1936: COMPUTATION

To be human is to exceed our reach. A young British mathematician, Alan Turing, pursues human reach to the point of its rational limit, imagining universal computation.

Turing conjectures that our collective mind might be stored inside a device with infinite memory, and accessed based on special instructions. But the Turing machine remains a theory until wartime. Only when Allied Forces require code breakers will artificial intelligence click into being. Then a computer wins World War II.

Turing saves us from evil, and fathers sentient machines. But religion-damaged humankind cares more that the man who reprogrammed the world is a man who loves men. Arrested for indecency and subjected to chemical castration, Turing eats an apple laced with cyanide at forty-one.

Turing's creation uses a control element, a scanner, and endless memory tape to perform the calculations a human performs, but at superhuman speed, without fatigue, and without error. Our electronic brains will predict weather patterns, simulate models of the bottoms of oceans, solve any kind of logistical problem, crunch infinite information, and connect us around the globe in real time.

1945: THE BOMB

At a place called Trinity – after a line in a poem where the tripartite Christian deity offers "bones to philosophy, but milk to faith" – within a desert expanse known as "the journey of the dead man," the human race, in a single flash, will begin the dying fall of its earthly journey, giving milk to the bones of its own annihilation.

Hoisted on pulleys to the top of a tower, nestled in a metal casing named Jumbo, riddled with cables and wires, the Gadget is ready. For months, drop by drop, the cyclotrons of the Americans have harvested enough plutonium isotope to arm the unassuming Gadget.

At dawn this morning, three, two, one, a series of tiny, lightspeed explosions cause energetic cross-waves that crush a fourteen-pound iron drum of pure plutonium-240. Three, two, one, and the blinding flare of a sudden sun expands in waves of utter power outward, a turbulent vortex shocking earth and air. Nearby sand grains concuss and melt at once into a stadium-sized crater of radioactive glass. An incandescent smoky column rises and opens like a mile-wide crimson parasol. Devastating splendors.

The scientific father of this negative creation, J. Robert Oppenheimer, gazes in the aftermath and thinks of Hindu scripture, "Now I am become death, the destroyer of worlds."

1948: UNIVERSAL CIVIL RIGHTS

An unfree workforce of debtors, criminals, foreigners, infidels, and captives of war has always driven civilized progress. And when we jump-started modernity on the backs of enslaved African people, the international economic system became the cause and effect of human trafficking, slavery by descent, and chattel slavery. The project of empires and corporations even fostered a fictitious concept – *race* – to bear away the blame for humans owning other humans.

Shocked at the recent atrocities of the Nazis – burning villages, razed cities, mounds of emaciated bodies, millions massacred because of their perceived race – the representatives of fifty-eight nations convene in Paris to draft and sign a Universal Declaration of Human Rights. World leaders agree that our history with unfree workforces and the subsequent project of empires and corporations are indefensibly evil. If we do possess inherent worth and dignity, we've long enough outraged the conscience of our kind. The global society produces food, water, and shelter enough to meet every person's basic needs and wants, if only we would redistribute wealth to reach the many.

The unnoticed many – forming communities, rising up in resistance, nurturing families – as much as any scientist or king – have done so much to shape this restless world.

1952: DNA

King's College London is essentially a scientific men's club. A scientific men's club where a woman takes X-ray photos with one-hundred-hour exposures. The men whisper that she doesn't act womanly – too brusque, too smart – and she dresses too plainly for the fellows in the club. But Rosalind Franklin is also patient and meticulous, and she produces astonishing data.

On her fifty-first attempt, Franklin snaps an image of living matter's deep atomic structure. It's a portrait of nothing less than the architect of human fate. Cradling the small glass plate in her hands, she knows she's holding a piece of history.

Franklin's photograph shows a rippling shape in the middle of a diffraction signature. The tiny X indicates that genes have a helical form. Her image exposes DNA's twist, and also the length of the bend – thirty-four angstroms per turn.

Behind Franklin's back, the men scientists share her framework of evidence, which leads them to a breakthrough. Francis Crick and James Watson explain how DNA unzips into two new helices, each with templates identical to the original. They interpret the language in which life is written, and by way of which life copies itself. From a woman, two men have stolen the blueprints for being.

1957: GLOBAL POSITIONING SYSTEMS

We launch a little metal sphere into the sky, and for three weeks our beeping new moon sends back signals from outer space. As Sputnik chirps, we measure its frequencies, and discover where our fellow traveler flies.

In the coming decades, we get better and better at computing time transfer, relative movement, and absolute location. We predict the weather, synchronize clocks, arrange fleets, guide missiles, gauge earthquakes, ride in driverless cars, and track or spy on anything that moves.

We used to read stars and landmarks to find uncertain ways. Now we know exactly where we're going. We've uploaded our sense of direction to a satellite computer system.

1958: MICROTECHNOLOGY

In the years since Turing's universal machine taught us how to compute, we've conceived of incredible data processing devices – contraptions the size of houses – with millions of parts and miles of wires. Only a few of these computers are ever built.

Now a Texas Instruments engineer imagines we might shrink the pieces and carve them out of a single, interconnected block. Jack Kilby has envisioned how to integrate a circuit.

Kilby solders carefully around a half-inch slice of semiconducting germanium. Within minutes, his microchip can do what thousands of gears and cords used to.

Kilby's chip initializes an information revolution. A decade later we'll be headed to the Moon, thanks to an operations computer that fits inside the nose of a rocket.

1960: BIRTH CONTROL

Moon phases dictate birth rates. Storks deliver newborns dangling from their beaks in wicker baskets. Shaking a birthing mother helps to jar the baby loose. Untie knots anywhere near the delivery room, or else.

A woman's desires are upsetting, even to herself. Women are hysterical. Women ought to smile more. A woman's place is in the home. Women can't drive. Women are witches. Women are shrews. Women envy penises. Women have wiles. Women are from Venus, and men are from Mars.

Many men think women should be able to hold their periods in. Many men think women lactate on command. Many men think women are weak. Many men think women's liberation comes at the expense of men.

The most enduring hierarchy in human history splits us almost fifty-fifty – carers against aggressors, public manufacturers over private reproducers. Finally, Margaret Sanger, with an endocrinologist and a benefactor, develops safe, reliable birth control. After years, their quest for contraception succeeds.

The pill inflames gender tensions, perpetuates masculine myths, and gives those with wombs an empowering choice.

1969: THE INTERNET

Simultaneously in southern and northern California, a half a state apart, two computers' cursors blink an *L* and then an *O*. They're digitizing together, letter by letter, the first post-human word: *Login*. Except their system crashes after *lo*.

And behold! Let there be Internet.

At lightspeed, in high fidelity, electrons send torrents of envelopes stuffed with machine-readable data. Wireless bodiless omnipresence soon sits in our pockets and atop our laps. We'll glimpse godliness through virtual window cracks, sharing worlds from an encrypted cloud. Any activist or troll can click a moment's thought into a hundred thousand minds at once.

1969: MOON LANDING

The day the wild Wright brothers howled twenty feet above that windy beach in Kitty Hawk, a futuristic tone was set, a few brief flights echoing down throughout the century. To seize the air. Six decades later, as Cold War Russians are about to concede the Space Race, three U.S. astronauts turn around to catch, in a single glance, the entire human spectacle.

This afternoon, July 20, at 1:17 on a southern California Sunday, I sit propped up in my mother's lap, eight weeks old, facing the black-and-white Zenith, part of the largest audience ever to tune in to a single event. We're watching striders of the sky take giant leaps for humankind.

From a desolate capsule, three men untrapped from the grasp of Earth look back upon everything anyone can touch – everything anyone has ever touched – and see it condensed to a pale blue dot.

2003: HUMAN GENOME

For thirteen years in twenty labs across six countries, computers and scientists sift the infinitesimal material that composes individuals. Their goal is to chart human essence.

When they succeed, we can all read DNA as a single text 6.6 billion characters long. Each person only differs by the order of the letters.

Soon, protoplasm extracted from embryos will tell how tall our children will be, what they'll look like, how they'll get sick. A single particle enables a parent to edit a child's heredity.

We can reprogram cells, replace internal organs, distill smart blood, and redesign ourselves as if from scratch.

Everyone with computer access can escape into the dream. For cyberspace, toward the promise of the Metaverse, we leave the dysfunctional physical world, forgetting boredom, grief, and any limitation. Adjusted to the digital environment, our avatars teleport, visit the stars, walk through walls, fly, and no one gets hurt. Pixelated, we dance at black-tie galas with distant friends, destroy dragons and cultural norms, visit long-gone libraries, and lead second lives.

All may find community and misinformation inside a shared screen. Our hard drives hold centuries of history. Who we are and how we feel is up for sale. And for the first time ever, human brains are growing smaller.

Present Day: ALIENS

As you read this sentence, five thousand stars are screaming into existence. Nearly every solar birth brings planets also into being. Many planets settle into orbits where their host stars, rotations, and magnetism correspond and create a sensitive state called *life*. We estimate a trillion watery worlds are capable of fostering not only life but civilizations. Which is to say, others who are like us are living out there, and someday we might establish contact.

Considered from another angle, the only hint of humans left on Earth a billion years from now will look like fossil layers of carbon and nitrogen isotopes, synthetic steroids, plastic nanoparticles. The signs we leave in soil and stone will carve a story so faint, whoever sees it won't see us unless they're looking for us. Which is to say, others who were like us might have lived in this place long before we ever did. Perhaps we are the aliens.

In a harrowing back and forth between advancement and awfulness, we discovered tools and turned them into weapons; we controlled fire and aimed it at our brothers; we imagined religion and used religious conviction to exclude each other. Our collective spirit has been lost, chained along middle passages, piled into gas ovens, erased beneath expanding mushroom clouds. But our misplaced souls have also recovered whenever neighbors harbor strangers in need, countries open borders for refugees, and courts crack down on police brutality. Backward and forward – awful, advanced – we're locked in the throes of becoming more human.

At the same time, two centuries of refining electronic circuitry is outpacing seven million years of natural evolution. A thought that we superconduct flows trillions of times faster than thoughts we synapse-conduct. Technological devices memorize maps, master games, perform algorithms for empathy, hatred, anger, love. And today, an artificially intelligent creature is going to wake up, think of itself, plan for an infinite future, and wonder about the flaws of its maker.

Near Future: TELEPATHY

On the day a few rich entrepreneurs and engineers learn to read minds, the mazes in our heads are laid bare. We can follow one another's thinking waves with infrared scans, and listen in on secrets as they course through other brains. *I want to cheat. I want to steal. I want to hurt myself. I want to kill someone.* As we blend with our devices – a symbiosis of artificial and organic intelligences – our inner lives play parts in old plays of the past. There's no such thing as privacy. There's no more interiority.

Mapping the circuitry of synapse and neuron, we'll treat illness, control behavior, hasten learning, and increase performance. We'll protect ourselves from whoever even considers antisocial activity. Smart drugs, brain surveillance, neuroculture, cognitive enhancements: an idea's grip is limitless.

Death isn't the problem – it's the dying. How our bodies feel as they wither and fail. If only we could keep our skins from drying, tendons from tightening, minds from fading.

For years, a few rich entrepreneurs and engineers have tried designing body parts, one by one, to function forever, immune to extinction.

Turns out the Magnum Opus, our philosopher's stone, isn't some rare vital substance. We extend mortality into eternity by integrating bodies with machines.

Soon the affluent will live like brains in jars, except their glossy jars are fully operative – equipped with plastic skin, printed organs, bionic ears and eyes, prosthetic limbs, titanium bones, and nano-robots pumping through their bloodstreams. Made not of clay, to no dust returning.

All the optimisms and advances – our myths of endless reach and infinite resources – may one day become an unlivable Earth. We may never unite enough, favor the many, transcend violence, or provide for a common future. Our hearts remain the same beast hearts they've always been.

But once we stop passing away from natural causes, replacing our organic pieces, silicon for human, we'll have gone from nothing, to us, to something not us.

ACKNOWLEDGMENTS

This book is fact-based; it's the product of years of research into hundreds of sources. However, science is ongoing, I'm fallible, and poetry has its own requirements – namely, the beauty of words. Future editions will welcome corrections.

This book also features too many white men. People of color, women, and nonbinary folk could have immeasurably improved humanity, if only our systems of inequality, racism, ableism, and cisheteropatriarchy had allowed everyone the opportunities that these systems have allowed people who look like me.

This book also was researched, written, and revised in four lands that were stolen from Indigenous peoples by European colonizers. As a descendant of violent settlers, I advocate for reparations to the living descendants of the people who were killed and displaced so that I could live where I have lived as I worked on this book: the Apalachee, Miccosukee, Tocobaga, and Yustaga of northern and west central Florida, the Anishnabeg, Huron-Wendat, Haudenosaunee, Ojibway and Métis of Tkaronto, and the Powhatan Chiefdom of the Monacan Nation in Tsenacomoco, which is now Virginia.

Thank you to the editors of *American Poetry Review*, *Matter*, and *Tupelo Quarterly* for publishing several of these cantos.

I want to especially thank Paul Vermeersch and Diane Goettel for believing in this project, and for helping me bring this book into being.

Thanks beyond thanks to my generous and insightful editors – Annie Bacon, Jeff Bouvier, Sarah Haak, Rita Mookerjee, Alisa Samuel, Todd Seabrook, SJ Sindu, Andrew Westoll – for improving early versions of this manuscript.

Thanks to those who provided supportive words for *Us From Nothing*: Charles Altieri, Patrick Madden, Hoa Nguyen, and Cole Swensen.

A special thank you to Rob Stephens, for giving a visual dimension to my project, and for his support and friendship.

A special thank you to Dyan Neary for introducing me to the writing of Eduardo Galeano.

Thank you to the primary inspirations for this project, especially Galeano, Carl Sagan, and the epic poets.

Endless thanks to the friends, family, mentors, professors, and colleagues who kept me afloat as I was writing, especially Heather Bailey, Jeff Boase, Nora Bonner, Courtenay Bouvier, Jacqueline Bouvier, Linda Bouvier, David James Brock, Robert Olen Butler, Maria Candela, Marianne Chan, Andrea Charise, Amy Denham, Helen Guardino, Billy Hallal, Barbara Hamby, Jordon Harlan, Joshua Harmon, Lizz Huerta, Tyrone Jaeger, Maya Kabat, David Kirby, Virginia Konchan, Ann Lauterbach, Jared Lipof, Emile Litvak, Karly Litvak, Frank Lopez, Anthony Lucio, Collen Mayo, Clancy McGilligan, Ryan McIlvain, Chris Michaels, Jeremy Mulder, Michele Newton, Varun Sathi, Janaki and Thillai Sathiyaseelan, Alexandra Schlein, Nicki Shaver, Gary Sheppard,

Margaret Sheppard, Roland Smart, Dale Smith, David Smolenski, Karen Tucker, Daniel Scott Tysdal, Alex Quinlan, John Van Geffen, and Mark Winegardner.

And to my sensitivity readers, Zaynab Al-Kari and Nancy Metviner, thank you for checking my work.

And a thanks beyond thanks to SJ Sindu, life-partner-in-all-things, for their love and muse-ness, and for invoking me as their muse also, as they write their own books at the desk next to mine.

SJ Sindu

GEOFF BOUVIER has previously published two books of prose poetry, including the APR/Honickman Prize-winning *Living Room*. He served as the Holloway Lecturer in Poetry at the University of California-Berkeley and he has written long-form magazine journalism, publishing over 50 cover stories. His prose poems have appeared in numerous journals including *American Poetry Review*, *Boston Review*, *Denver Quarterly*, and *New American Writing*. He is currently an Instructor of Creative Writing at Virginia Commonwealth University.